CRAFT BEER
FOR THE HOMEBREWER

RECIPES FROM AMERICA'S
TOP BREWMASTERS

MICHAEL AGNEW

WITH BILLY BROAS, DENNY CONN,
MATTHEW SCHAEFER & JORDAN WIKLUND

Voyageur Press

First published in 2014 by Voyageur Press, an imprint of Quarto Publishing Group USA Inc.,
400 First Avenue North, Suite 400, Minneapolis, MN 55401 USA

Voyageur Press titles are also available at discounts in bulk quantity for industrial or sales-promotional
use. For details write to Special Sales Manager at Quarto Publishing Group USA Inc., 400 First Avenue North,
Suite 400, Minneapolis, MN 55401 USA.

To find out more about our books, visit us online at www.voyageurpress.com.

ISBN: 978-0-7603-4474-3

Library of Congress Cataloging-in-Publication Data

Agnew, Michael.
   Craft beer for the homebrewer : recipes from America's top brewmasters / Michael Agnew with Billy
Broas, Denny Conn, Matthew Schaefer, and Jordan Wiklund.
      pages cm
   Includes index.
   ISBN 978-0-7603-4474-3 (hardcover)
   1. Brewing--Amateurs' manuals 2. Beer--Amateurs' manuals 3. Microbreweries--United States. I. Title.
II. Title: Craft beer for the home brewer.
   TP577.A35 2014
   663'.42--dc23
                        2013025400

Frontis: jeka84 (www.shutterstock.com)
Opposite: LICreate (www.istockphoto.com)

Acquisitions Editor: Dennis Pernu
Design Manager: Cindy Samargia Laun
Cover Design: Matt Simmons
Interior Design: Mary Rohl
Layout: Mandy Kimlinger

Printed in China

CONTENTS

INTRODUCTION

Ask any professional brewers how they got their start and you are likely to hear the words, "Well, I started homebrewing." Indeed, homebrewing is the source from which the current U.S. beer culture has sprung. America's first microbrewery, New Albion Brewing Company, in Sonoma, California, was founded in 1976 by Jack McAuliffe, a homebrewer. Ken Grossman of Sierra Nevada and Jim Koch of Sam Adams both started as homebrewers. Today, homebrewers remain a vital force in the industry, providing inspiration, audience, and a deep well of new talent.

The industry hasn't forgotten its roots. Individual brewers and the breweries where they work regularly and generously give back to the homebrewing community. They open their facilities for club meetings and competitions. Many are willing to make field calls from questioning homebrewers seeking troubleshooting advice or tips to help them make better beer. Some breweries reward homebrewers with the opportunity to brew their medal-winning beers on a commercial scale and then offer them for sale in the taproom or pub. Perhaps the ultimate expression of this is the ProAm Competition at the annual Great American Beer Festival, where professional brewers collaborate with award-winning homebrewers and enter the resulting beers in a special category at what is one of the world's largest brewing competitions.

This book is a manifestation of that desire to give back. It is also a testament to the high degree of openness and camaraderie that exists in the industry. Cooperation between competitors is rare in the business world, but it is the norm among America's small brewers. Exchanging information, insights, and even raw materials is commonplace. Collaborative brews are a growing trend, and what more obvious sign of this openness could you find than the willingness to allow recipes to be published in a book for national distribution? The beers produced are each brewery's lifeblood.

Yet here they are, described in detail for use by homebrewers everywhere. What other industry does that? You'll never see Coca-Cola or PepsiCo releasing their formulas to the public.

Perhaps this says something about the nature of beer. Beer is and always has been a catalyst for social connection. In his great book, *Uncorking the Past*, archaeologist Patrick McGovern lays out evidence showing that beer was a central part of the social and ritual life of many ancient cultures. Cultivating barley for brewing may have been one spark that led to the development of settled, agrarian civilizations. In more modern times we have the well-established tradition of "going 'round the pub" for a pint (or three) with friends. And every homebrewer knows that an important part of each brewing session is gathering friends around the kettle to watch liquid boil while enjoying some homemade brew. Everywhere you look, beer brings people together.

It's a great time to be a homebrewer. The hobby is exploding. In May 2013 Alabama became the last state to legalize homebrewing. That same month, the American Homebrewers Association (AHA) listed 1,485 clubs, more than double the number from 2008. Nearly 3,400 people attended the 2012 National Homebrewers Conference, compared to 950 in 2008. The 2012 National Homebrew Competition registered 8,000 entries.

These are boom times for commercial brewers as well. According to the AHA, there were 2,416 breweries operating in the United States in March 2013, the most since the late nineteenth century. The AHA lists nearly 1,300 more breweries in planning. Craft beer production volume and sales have increased by double-digit percentages every year since 2010, bringing the craft sector to more than 6 percent of the total U.S. beer market. The vibrant creativity of American brewers has started to infect the rest of the world.

It's hard to talk about "writing" a book like this. We didn't create the recipes. That credit belongs to the brewers who applied their skills and expertise to craft the beers we love to drink and would like to brew. We did adjust some recipes, though, to ensure that they fit our standardization specifications. Those specifications provide an important baseline. Every brewer's system and process produces different results. Some will extract more sugar from the grains. Others deliver better utilization of the bitter alpha acids in hops. This variation makes it essential to know the basic assumptions on which a recipe is built. To get the best results from this book, use the standardized recipes as a starting point and then tweak them to fit your own system, process, and ingredients.

A digital kitchen scale capable of measuring fractions of ounces is a must for the recipes in this book! At the homebrew level, small variances can yield dramatically different profiles.
Jess mine (www.shutterstock.com)

Even with standardization, these system variables and other things such as water composition or fermenter geometry make it difficult for homebrewers to replicate their favorite beers exactly. Use this book as a way to get close. It's fun to compare your results to the real thing and evaluate the differences. As your brewing skills advance and you learn the quirks of your equipment you can further hone the recipes to zero in on your target.

As you embark on brewing these recipes, a few equipment upgrades will help you get closer to the mark. A digital kitchen scale capable of measuring fractions of ounces is a must, as scaling down hop additions sometimes leaves you with odd amounts. At the homebrew level, small variances can yield dramatically different profiles. Invest in a means of controlling fermentation temperatures. Most of the flaws detected in homebrew competition entries are fermentation related. Being able to precisely control fermentation will be a big step toward making better beer. There are a number of options available. Check with your favorite homebrew store to find the one that is best for your situation.

Finally, a wort aeration tool is a good investment. Yeast health is critically important, and yeast needs oxygen to grow at the start of fermentation. While the tried-and-true shaking method works, it's hard work to hoist and shake 5 gallons of wort for the amount of time needed to be effective. In fact, it can be downright dangerous if you ferment in glass. Again, there are many options available.

Now get brewing!

—Michael Agnew, May 2013

byggarn.se (www.shutterstock.com)

RECIPE STANDARDIZATION

Batch size: 5 gal.

Extract efficiency: 65%

(One lb. of two-row malt with a potential extract value of 1.037 in 1 gal. of water yields wort of 1.024.)

Extract values for malt extract: LME (liquid malt extract) = 1.033–1.037

DME (dry malt extract) = 1.045

Potential extract for grains: Two-row base malt = 1.037–1.038

Six-row base malt = 1.035

Wheat malt = 1.037

Munich malt = 1.035

Vienna malt = 1.035

Crystal malt = 1.033–1.035

Chocolate malt = 1.034

Dark-roasted grains = 1.024–1.026

Flaked corn and rice = 1.037–1.038

Hops: The IBU (international bitterness units) is calculated on 25% utilization for a one-hour boil of hop pellets at SG of 1.050.

Process: Extract recipes assume steeping specialty grains at 160°F for 30 minutes at a rate of 0.5 gal. of water to 0.5 lb. of grain, followed by a 60-minute boil with full extract, and then primary fermentation until final gravity is reached, followed by a one-week conditioning period in a separate vessel. Deviations from this process, such as late extract additions, are indicated in the recipe instructions.

All-grain recipes assume a 60-minute, single-infusion mash, sparge at 170°F, a 60-minute boil, and then primary fermentation until final gravity is reached, followed by a one-week conditioning period in a separate vessel. Deviations from this process, such as stepped mash, are indicated in the recipe instructions.

1

PALE ALES & IPAS

Hops! The bitter and the spice of beer. No style better showcases hops than pale ale. And no one does pale ale better than American craft brewers. Hoppy pale ales have been central to the craft beer movement since the late 1970s. Arguably, the first American craft beer was New Albion Ale from New Albion Brewing Company, a pale that would seem mild by today's standards but which was a hop bomb in its day. Since then, American brewers have pushed the envelope of hoppiness with super-aromatic beers that pump the International Bittering Units (IBUs) to palate-testing proportions. Heaps of hops are now the signature of American beer.

Highly hopped beers have been around since at least the thirteenth century. Hops first arrived in England in the 1400s. Recognizing the preservative quality of hops, English brewers began making strong, hoppy beers meant for long aging. Pale ale made its first appearance at the turn of the eighteenth century when advances in the malting process allowed the production of lighter colored malts. "Pale" here was a relative term insomuch as these amber-colored brews were lighter than the brown beers that were the norm. When these pale beers were shipped to the English colonies, the gentle back-and-forth motion of the ship during months-long voyages roused the yeast in the casks, kicking off a secondary fermentation. The result was a drier beer that accentuated the hops. Thus the India pale ale (IPA) was born. Changing palates and war-related shortages caused IPAs to evolve into the more sessionable pale ales (or "bitters") that are still the centerpiece of English brewing today.

To satisfy craft brewers' demand for exciting flavors and aromas, hop growers are developing new varieties all the time. It can be helpful, though, to have familiarity with the traditional growing regions and the character of the hops they produce. American hops, grown mostly in the Pacific Northwest, tend toward citrusy, floral, or piney flavors. English varieties are generally grassy, earthy, and herbal, with subtle citrus notes. Hops from continental Europe, such as the classic Saaz hop, lean more toward perfume and spice with undertones of blackberries and currants.

While hops are king, balance should not be forgotten when brewing pale ales and IPAs. It's tempting to think only about the hops, but keep the malt in mind. Bitterness needs a bit of malty sweetness to back it up. The tangerine and grapefruit citrus of many American hops taste heavenly against a backdrop of caramel and biscuit. Keep in mind that IBUs can be deceptive. These are a chemical measurement of the isomerized alpha acids in beer. Perceived bitterness may be different. Factors such as residual sugar can make two beers with similar IBU ratings seem to have very different levels of bitterness.

8-Bit
Tallgrass Brewing Company, Manhattan, Kansas

Tallgrass Brewing Company's pale ale 8-Bit was inspired by 1980s videogames. Crude by today's standards, those games are nonetheless fun to play and still offer a challenge. This beer is a throwback to the classic pale ales that kicked off the American beer renaissance in the 1980s. It's light, crisp, moderately bitter, and easy to drink. But if you push beneath the seemingly simple surface, you find flavors that will tickle the taste buds of even the biggest beer nerd. "The thing that really makes this beer stand out from the other pale ales are the Galaxy hops that we use to dry hop this beer," says Tallgrass head brewer Andrew Hood. "They add a lot of different fruit notes to the beer. Some that I pick up are cantaloupe, honeydew, and other melon-type fruits."

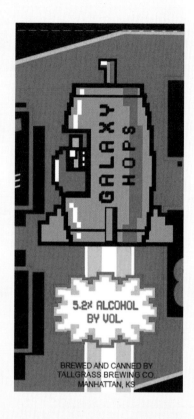

SPECIFICATIONS	OG: 1.052	FG: 1.013	ABV: 5.2%	IBU: 35—40	SRM: 6.5

Crush and steep the following ingredients in 1.25 gal. (4.7 L) of water at 160°F (71°C) for 30 minutes:

- 9.6 oz. (272 g) Briess Goldpils Vienna malt
- 5.6 oz. (159 g) Briess Dark Munich malt
- 4.8 oz. (136 g) Briess Victory malt

Strain the grain into your brewpot and sparge with .5 gal. (2 L) of water at 160°F (71°C). Bring the wort to a boil, remove from the heat, and add:

- 6 lb. (2.7 kg) light liquid malt extract
- 8 oz. (225 g) light dry malt extract

Stir well until the extract is completely dissolved. Add water as needed to bring the total volume to 3 gal. (11.3 L). Bring the wort to a rolling boil. Boil for 15 minutes and then add:

- .5 oz. (14 g) Magnum hop pellets (14% AA)

Boil for 30 minutes and then add:

- .3 oz. (8.5 g) Centennial hop pellets (10.5% AA)

Boil for 15 minutes and then add:

- .3 oz. (8.5 g) Cascade hop pellets (6% AA)
- .15 oz. (4.2 g) Willamette hop pellets (5.5% AA)

Remove from the heat and then add:

- .1 oz. (2.8 g) Willamette hop pellets (5.5% AA)
- .2 oz. (5.7 g) Cascade hop pellets (6% AA)

Rest for 10 minutes and then add:

- 1.1 oz. (31 g) Centennial hop pellets (10.5% AA)

Rest for 10 minutes and then chill the wort as quickly as possible to below 80°F (27°C), using an ice bath or wort chiller. Transfer the wort to the fermenter and add cold water to bring the total volume to 5 gal. (19 L). Aerate the wort. Add the yeast:

- Wyeast 1450 Denny's Favorite

Ferment at 68°F (20°C) until final gravity is achieved. Perform a diacetyl rest by raising the temperature to 70°F (21°C) for 48 hours. Siphon to a secondary fermenter and add:

- 2.5 oz. (71 g) Galaxy whole-leaf hops (13% AA)

Allow the beer to condition for 5 to 7 days. Bottle when fermentation is complete with:

- 6 oz. (170 g) corn sugar

ALL-GRAIN INSTRUCTIONS

Replace the malt extract with 9.9 lb. (4.5 kg) of Briess two-row brewer's malt. Crush the grains, and mash at 152°F (67°C) for 60 minutes. Raise the temperature to 170°F (77°C), and rest for 10 minutes. Sparge with 170°F (77°C) water until you reach a total volume 6 gal. (22.7 L) in the brewpot. Reduce the 60-minute Magnum hop addition to .4 oz. (11 g). Reduce the 30-minute Centennial hop addition to .25 oz. (7 g). Reduce the 15-minute Cascade hop addition to .25 oz. (7 g). Reduce the 15-minute Willamette hop addition to .1 oz. (3 g).

TALLGRASS BREWING COMPANY
MANHATTAN, KANSAS

YOU KNOW THE MAXIM: Behind every good homebrewer is a patient spouse. At least, that's the story for Jeff Gill, founder and brewer of Tallgrass Brewing Company. In 2006, his wife, Tricia, asked him just what it is he'd really like to do with his life. The answer was simple: start a microbrewery.

After six years of homebrewing, Gill realized he valued the process of crafting and enjoying homebrew more than his day job as an environmental geologist. Thus, with a little support from his wife, the dream of owning and operating a brewery was born. Just one year later, Tallgrass debuted Pub Ale, a mild English ale, and since then Tallgrass has churned out an impressive array of different styles of beer, from light to dark, hoppy to heavy, Velvet Rooster (a light, Belgian-style Tripel) to Buffalo Sweat (a dark, oatmeal cream stout).

Located in Manhattan, Kansas, in the northeastern part of the state, Tallgrass draws inspiration from the landscape around it and the goal of "bringing people together over a great beer." The rolling fields of America's Midwest provide the perfect backdrop for a brewery, as a wide variety of grains and cereals are readily available for brewing.

Recently, Tallgrass has issued an all-purpose "Canifesto." After receiving a call from a Tallgrass aficionado who wanted to return twenty boxes of empty bottles, Gill knew he had a responsibility as a former geologist to do something about the sustainability of his products. Because cans completely block UV sunrays and seal better than beer in bottles, Gill made the decision to distribute only cans instead of bottles. According to the Canifesto, cans are also more fun, more mobile, and easier to recycle. The turnover from a recycled can to a new one on the shelf is just sixty days.

Tallgrass beer can be found in many stores, bars, and restaurants in fourteen states in the middle of the country, stretching from Montana in the West to Alabama in the South and everywhere in between. With luck (and thirsty customers), that number will grow as Tallgrass' reputation for high-quality, delicious beer continues to spread. —*Jordan Wiklund*

Capt'n Crompton's Pale Ale

Epic Brewing, Salt Lake City, Utah

When the alcohol laws in Utah were loosened in 2008, some longtime self-described beer geeks saw their opportunity to follow their passions and opened Epic Brewing. Capt'n Crompton's Pale Ale leads Epic's Classic Series of "not-so-basic, basic" brews designed to give your "taste adventure" a "jumping-off point." Capt'n Crompton's is designed to drink smooth and be well balanced with an aroma and flavor dominated by classic Pacific Northwest hops. —*Matthew Schaefer*

SPECIFICATIONS	OG: 1.061	FG: 1.016	ABV: 5.9%	IBU: 38	SRM: 9

Crush and steep in 2 gal. (7.5 L) of water at 160°F (71°C) for 30 minutes:

- 8 oz. (225 g) Carapils malt
- 8 oz. (225 g) Caramunich malt

Strain the grain into your brewpot, and sparge with .5 gallon (2 L) of water at 160°F (71°C). Bring the water to a boil, remove from the heat, and add:

- 3.15 lb. (1.43 kg) Maris Otter liquid malt extract
- 3.65 lb. (1.65 kg) light dry malt extract

Stir well until the extract is completely dissolved. Add water to bring the total volume to 3 gal. (11.3 L). Bring the wort to a rolling boil and then add:

- .75 oz. (21.26 g) Centennial hop pellets (10.5% AA)

Boil for 30 minutes and then add:

- .5 oz. (14.17 g) Mount Hood hop pellets (5% AA)

Boil for 25 minutes and then add:

- .3 oz. (8.5 g) Amarillo hop pellets (9.5% AA)
- .3 oz. (8.5 g) Cascade hop pellets (6% AA)

Boil for 5 more minutes, remove from the heat, chill the wort as quickly as possible to below 80°F (27°C), using an ice bath or wort chiller. Transfer the wort to the fermenter and add cold water to bring the total volume to 5 gal. (19 L). Aerate the wort. Add the yeast:

- White Labs WLP051 California Ale V

Ferment at 68°F (20°C) until final gravity is achieved. Siphon to a secondary fermenter and dry hop for seven days with:

- 1 oz. (28 g) Cascade hop pellets (6% AA)

Bottle when fermentation is complete with:

- 5 oz. (140 g) corn sugar

ALL-GRAIN INSTRUCTIONS

Replace the malt extract with 6.5 lb. (2.95 kg) of Marris Otter malt and 5 lb. (2.25 kg) of two-row malt. Crush the grains and mash at 152° F (67° C) for 60 minutes. Sparge with 170°F (79°C) water to reach a total volume of 6.5 gal. (24.6 L) in the brewpot for a 90-minute boil. Reduce the 60-minute Centennial hop addition to .6oz. (17 g) and reduce the 30-minute Mount Hood hops addition to .4 oz. (11.34 g).

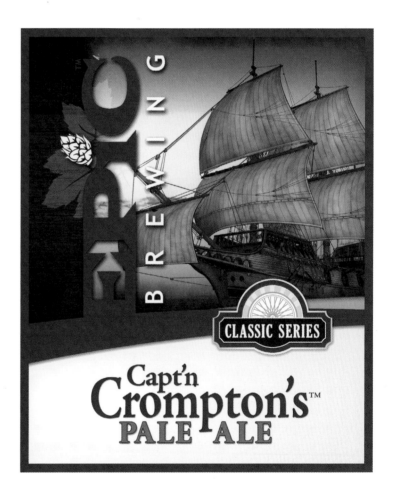

Elevated IPA
La Cumbre Brewing Company, Albuquerque, New Mexico

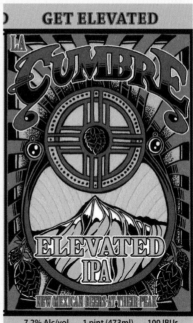

In 2009, master brewer Jeff Erway left his position as a music teacher to open La Cumbre Brewing Co. in Albuquerque, New Mexico. Two years later, he walked away with a gold medal at the Great American Brewing Festival with his flagship beer, Elevated IPA. To call this beer a "hop bomb" would be an understatement and a disservice to the intricate web of flavors brought about through the use of four types of hops over the course of five hop additions. —*Matthew Schaefer*

PRO BREWER'S TIP

Pitch a proper amount of yeast, oxygenate to 12 ppm, and maintain fermentation temperatures. Pitching too little yeast will result in a beer with excessive fermentation characteristics. Pitching too much yeast will result in the stripping out of iso-alpha acids and will make a less bitter beer. There's nothing wrong with today's dried yeast for homebrewers and you can be confident in pitching one rehydrated pack of US-05.

The batch of IPA that won gold at the 2011 Great American Beer Festival was brewed twelve days before bottling. *Do not age this beer in any way, shape, or form.* Dry hop in a sealed container if at all possible. Cornelius kegs work well for this purpose. Use Biofine Clear to get a quickly servable IPA with good clarity.

The hop varieties change for this beer constantly. The Columbus you get this year may be big and piney and next year weak and reeking of garlic and onions. Be open to interpretation and change and always make the best IPA you can. Using a blend of a number of hops helps in mitigating varietal drift between one year and another. Always know what you are going for and use your hop additions to get you there.

If the driest IPA is what you desire, try a Canadian pilsner base malt. While the color is far less than Crisp pale, there is far less husk material (contributing to a tannic wort) than with the American grown two-row. The flavor is incredibly pleasant but neutral.

SPECIFICATIONS	OG: 1.068	FG: 1.012	ABV: 7.2%	IBU: 100	SRM: 13

Crush and steep in 2 gal. (7.5 L) of water at 165°F (67°C) for 30 minutes:

- 9 oz. (340 g) Baird's Carastan 30L malt
- 1 oz. (28 g) Chinook hop pellets (13% AA)

Strain the grain into your brewpot and sparge with .5 gal. (2 L) of water at 160°F (71°C). Bring the water to a boil, remove from the heat, and add:

- 2 lb. (.9 kg) Maris Otter liquid malt extract
- 2 lb. (.9 kg) wheat liquid malt extract
- 5 lb. (2.26 kg) of Pilsen pilsner liquid malt extract

Stir well until the extract is completely dissolved. Add water to bring the total volume to 3 gal. (11.3 L). Bring the wort to a rolling boil and then add:

- 1.5 ml HopShot (hop extract)

Boil for 30 minutes and then add:

- 1 oz. (28 g) Columbus hop pellets (15% AA)

Boil for 15 minutes and then add:

- 1 oz. (28 g) Columbus hop pellets (15% AA)

Remove from the heat and add:

- 1 oz. (28 g) Nelson Sauvin hop pellets (12.5% AA)
- 1 oz. (28 g) Chinook hop pellets (13% AA)
- 1 oz. (28 g) Columbus hop pellets (15% AA)

Allow to rest for 30 minutes and then chill the wort as quickly as possible to below 80°F (27°C), using an ice bath or wort chiller. Transfer the wort to the fermenter and add cold water to bring the total volume to 5 gal. (19 L). Aerate the wort. Add yeast:

- Wyeast 1056 American Ale, White Labs WLP001 California Ale, or Safale US-05

Ferment at 62°F (17°C) until final gravity is achieved. Siphon to a secondary fermenter and allow the beer to condition for 7 to 10 days. Bottle when fermentation is complete with:

- 5 oz. (140 g) corn sugar

ALL-GRAIN INSTRUCTIONS

Replace the base malt extract with 12 lb. (5.44 kg) of Crisp Pale malt and 1.1 lb. (.49 kg) of wheat malt. Crush the grains and mash at 150°F (66°C) for 60 minutes. Sparge with 170°F (77°C) water until you reach a total volume of 6 gal. (22.7 L). Reduce the first wort Chinook hop addition to .82 oz. (23.24 g). Reduce the 30-minute and 15-minute Columbus hop additions to .82 oz. (23.24 g).

Troy Paff, The Journeyman Project (www.journeymanproject.net)

LA CUMBRE BREWING COMPANY

ALBUQUERQUE, NEW MEXICO

Troy Paff, The Journeyman Project (www.journeymanproject.net)

WHEN YOUR BREWERY'S MOTTO IS "New Mexican Beers at Their Peak," your beer better not disappoint. In 2011, Le Cumbre Brewing Company, of Albuquerque, New Mexico, lived up to its motto. The young brewery netted two gold medals and a silver at the Great American Beer Festival for American-Style India Pale Ale, American-Style or International-Style Pilsner, and a Foreign-Style Stout.

La Cumbre began as the dream of homebrewer Jeff Erway and his wife, Laura. They met over a beer and pursued their passion for suds across the country and eventually around the world, going so far as England and Belgium to hone their palates. As a teacher, Jeff wasn't able to pursue home brewing *every* day, but it weighed heavily on his mind. And after three hectic years of doing both, he decided to hang it up and get a job at Chama River Brewing Company, New Mexico's most successful brewery.

After a few more medals at the GABF with Chama, Jeff knew it was time. With Laura's support and encouragement, they opened La Cumbre Brewing Company and were soon garnering their own medals on the heels of Chama River Brewing Company. La Cumbre keeps five beers on tap throughout the year, including Elevated IPA, one of their gold-medal winners. Elevated boasts a 7.2 ABV rating and a whopping 100 IBUs. For those who enjoy darker beers, the silver-medal-winning Malpais Stout is also available as a taproom standby. Described as "a meal in a glass," seven different malts compose this hearty offering. Throughout the year, La Cumbre boasts a variety of seasonal and specialty beers as well.

La Cumbre means "summit" or "pinnacle" in Spanish. But when you start at the top, where else is there to go? Jeff and Laura are determined to find out. —*Jordan Wiklund*

Furious
Surly Brewing Company, Minneapolis, Minnesota

Surly Brewing Company broke onto the Twin Cities brewing scene in 2006 and almost immediately gained nationwide cult status. Surly regularly ranks near the top of the "Best Breweries" lists on popular rating sites like RateBeer.com and BeerAdvocate. While the brewery's reputation is for extremity, a glance at its full lineup reveals a softer side. The monstrous Darkness Imperial Stout shares the list with an English bitter, a Helles lager, and even an English mild ale. Surly's flagship Furious falls decidedly on the extreme side. It's typically listed as an IPA, but brewer Todd Haug has called it a West Coast–style red ale. Call it what you like, it's searingly bitter and bursting with pine and citrus hop flavor. It's definitely one for the hopheads.

SPECIFICATIONS	OG: 1.064	FG: 1.017	ABV: 6.2%	IBU: 99	SRM: 15

Crush these specialty grains and steep in 2.5 gal. (9.5 L) of water at 160°F (71°C) for 20 minutes:

- 12 oz. (340 g) English Medium Crystal malt
- 8 oz. (225 g) Belgian aromatic malt
- 2 oz. (57 g) English roasted barley
- .5 oz. (14 g) Amarillo hop pellets (9.5% AA)

Strain the grain into your brewpot. Bring the wort to a boil, remove from the heat, and add:

- 6.3 lb. (2.85 kg) light liquid malt extract

Stir well until the extract is completely dissolved. Add water as needed to bring the total volume to 3 gal. (11.3 L). Bring the wort to a rolling boil and add:

- 1.6 oz. (45.36 g) Warrior hop pellets (16% AA)

Boil for 45 minutes, remove from the heat, and then add:

- 2 lb. (.9 kg) light dry malt extract

Boil for another 15 minutes, remove from the heat and add:

- 2 oz. (57 g) Amarillo hop pellets (9.5% AA)

Chill the wort as quickly as possible to below 80°F (27°C), using an ice bath or wort chiller. Transfer the wort to the fermenter and add cold water to bring the total volume to 5.5 gal. (20.8 L). Aerate the wort. Add the yeast:

- Wyeast 1335 British Ale II

Ferment at 68°F (20°C) until final gravity is achieved. Siphon to a secondary fermenter and allow the beer to condition for 1 to 2 weeks. Add:

- 1 oz. (28.35 g) Warrior whole-leaf hops (16% AA)
- .25 oz. (7.08 g) Ahtanum whole-leaf hops (6% AA)
- .25 oz. (7.08 g) Amarillo whole-leaf hops (9.5% AA)
- .25 oz. (7.08 g) Simcoe whole-leaf hops (13% AA)

Allow the beer to condition for 1 to 2 weeks. Bottle when fermentation is complete with:

- 5 oz. (140 g) corn sugar

ALL-GRAIN INSTRUCTIONS

Replace the malt extract with 9.75 lb. (4.42 kg) Canada Malting Pale Ale malt and 4.75 lb. (2.15 kg) Simpsons Golden Promise malt. Crush the grains and mash at 153°F (67°C) for 60 minutes. Mash out at 168°F (76°C). Sparge with 170°F (77°C) water until you reach a total volume of 6.5 gal. (24.6 L) in the brewpot. Reduce the 60-minute Warrior hop addition to 1.2 oz. (34.2 g).

Hop Stoopid
Lagunitas Brewing Company, Petaluma, California

Lagunitas Brewing Company is known for its edgy and bracingly bitter beers. As the name suggests, Hop Stoopid lives up to this reputation: "It pours golden and looks friendly, but looks can be deceiving." This is how this beer is described in a virtual-taste video on the brewery's website. Indeed, Hop Stoopid is a true hop-head's delight. Hop aromas greet your nose without even raising the glass. Floral, fruit, and resinous flavors accompany pounding bitterness that is barely backed up by the malt. Note that the 321 IBU rating is a calculated number that bears little relation to reality. There are limitations to how much alpha acid can be absorbed into beer. Still, this is a crazy bitter beer.

SPECIFICATIONS	OG: 1.073	FG: 1.013	ABV: 8%	IBU: 321*	SRM: 5–6

*(CALCULATED)

Crush and steep the malt in .5 gal. (2 L) of water at 160°F (71°C) for 30 minutes:

- 8 oz. (225 g) Victory malt

Strain the grain into your brewpot and sparge with .5 gal. (2 L) of water at 160°F (71°C). Bring the wort to a boil, remove from the heat, and add:

- 9.15 lb. (4.15kg) light liquid malt extract
- 13.6 oz. (386 g) light dry malt extract
- 1 rounded tsp. (5 g) gypsum

Stir well until the extract is completely dissolved. Add water as needed to bring the volume to 3 gal. (11.3 L). Bring the wort to a rolling boil and add:

- 5 oz. (142 g) Columbus hop pellets (15% AA)

Boil for 78 minutes and then add:

- 1.2 oz. (34 g) Cascade hop pellets (6% AA)
- 1.2 oz. (34 g) Chinook hop pellets (13% AA)

Boil for 12 minutes, remove from the heat, and add:

- 2 oz. (57 g) Simcoe hop pellets (13% AA)

Chill the wort as quickly as possible to below 80°F (27°C), using an ice bath or wort chiller. Transfer the wort to the fermenter and add cold water to bring the total volume to 5 gal. (19 L). Aerate the wort. Add the yeast:

- WLP002 English Ale

Ferment at 65–68°F (18–20°C) until final gravity is achieved. Siphon to a secondary fermenter and add:

- 2.6 oz. (74 g) Columbus hop pellets (15% AA)
- 1.3 oz. (37 g) Simcoe hop pellets (13% AA)
- .65 oz. (18 g) Chinook hop pellets (13% AA)

Allow the beer to condition for 5 to 7 days. Bottle when fermentation is complete with:

- 6 oz. (170 g) corn sugar

ALL-GRAIN INSTRUCTIONS

Replace the malt extract with 15.2 lb. (6.9 kg) of two-row pale malt. Crush the grains and mash at 152°F (67°C) for 60 minutes. Add 2 rounded tsp. (10 g) of gypsum to the mash. Sparge with 170°F (77°C) water until you reach a total volume 6.5 gal. (24.6 L) in the brewpot. Reduce the 90-minute Columbus hop addition to 4.1 oz. (116 g). Reduce the 12-minute Cascade and Chinook hop additions to 1 oz. (28 g).

LAGUNITAS BREWING COMPANY
PETALUMA, CALIFORNIA

WHAT DO YOU GET WHEN YOU COMBINE the Pacific sea breeze, the northern California coast, and a bunch of laid-back brewers who draw inspiration from the likes of Steely Dan and other Laurel Canyon poets? Besides great music, you get a brewery like Lagunitas.

Established in Lagunitas, California, in 1993, the brewing company quickly outgrew its modest output and moved up the coast to Petaluma, sitting just off El Camino Real (the California-coast-cruisin' U.S. Route 101), north of San Francisco and west of Sacramento. Despite its modest and casual roots, as of 2010 Lagunitas boasts one of the largest distributions of microbreweries in the country, moving more than 106,000 barrels (3.3 million gallons) of beer from coast to coast in more than thirty states.

Lagunitas is definitely one of the more inspired breweries around. Its bottles and advertising often feature irreverent and whimsical messages. Lagunitas boasts an array of regular and seasonal styles and flavors, but the brewing company is known most for its refreshing and citrusy IPAs. Lagunitas wears its heart on its labels; for example, the label of Lagunitas Hop Stoopid double IPA cites the words from Steely Dan's "Kid Charlemagne," warning to "Clean this mess up else we'll all end up in jail . . . those test tubes and the scale . . . just get 'em all outta here!"

As the founding brewers of Lagunitas hailed from different locations around the country, part of Lagunitas' mission statement is to provide high-quality beer in a collaborative effort and produce a product that acts as a social lubricant among friends. Lucky for the brewing company, its message has been warmly received by beer drinkers near and far, and in 2012, Lagunitas announced the opening of another brewery in Chicago. Slated to open in 2013, the future of Lagunitas looks bright. —*Jordan Wiklund*

Maharaja
Avery Brewing Company, Boulder, Colorado

Avery Brewing Company sold its first beer in 1993, but the brewery didn't really catch on until 1996 when founder Adam Avery started pushing boundaries with bigger and bolder flavors. Avery has become a national leader in the realm of highly hopped and high-alcohol beers. The Maharaja is one of the beers that sealed that reputation. This IPA is bigger and bolder than most, but it's still nicely balanced. Its 102 IBUs of bitterness give it a brisk start that is followed by a blast of citrus and pine hop flavor. Underlying it all is a full and complex layer of sweet, caramel malt that keeps the hops under control.

Tobias Ott (www.istockphoto.com)

SPECIFICATIONS	OG: 1.090	FG: 1.012	ABV: 10.3%	IBU: 102	SRM: 13

Crush and steep the following in 1 gal. (3.8 L) of water at 160°F (71°C) for 30 minutes:

- 9 oz. (255 g) Victory malt
- 9 oz. (255 g) Crystal 120L malt

Strain the grain into your brewpot and sparge with .5 gal. (2 L) of water at 160°F (71°C). Add water as needed to bring the total volume to 1.5 gal. (5.7 L). Bring the water to a boil, remove from the heat, and add:

- 12 lb. (5.4 kg) light liquid malt extract

Stir well until the extract is completely dissolved. Add water to bring the total volume to 3 gal. (11.3 L). Bring the wort to a rolling boil then add:

- 1.3 oz. (36.85 g) Columbus hop pellets (15% AA)

Boil for 30 minutes and then add:

- 1.5 oz. (43 g) Columbus hop pellets (15% AA)

Boil for another 30 minutes, remove from the heat, and add:

- 2.2 oz. (62 g) Centennial hop pellets (10.5% AA)
- 2.2 oz. (62 g) Simcoe hop pellets (13% AA)

Chill the wort as quickly as possible to below 80°F (27°C), using an ice bath or wort chiller. Transfer the wort to the fermenter and add cold water to bring the total volume to 5 gal. (19 L). Aerate the wort. Add the yeast:

- Wyeast 1056 American Ale, WLP 001 California Ale, or Safale US-05

Ferment at 68°F (20°C) until final gravity is achieved. Siphon to a secondary fermenter and add:

- 4.4 oz. (125 g) Simcoe hop pellets (13% AA)
- 2.2 oz. (62 g) Centennial hop pellets (10.5% AA)
- 2.2 oz. (62 g) Chinook hop pellets (13% AA)

Allow the beer to condition for 7 to 10 days. Bottle when fermentation is complete with:

- 6 oz. (170 g) corn sugar

ALL-GRAIN INSTRUCTIONS

Replace the light liquid malt extract with 18 lb. (8.2 kg) pale two-row malt. Crush the grains and mash at 147°F (64°C) for 60 minutes. Sparge with 170°F (77°C) water until you reach a total volume 6 gal. (22.7 L) in the brewpot. Reduce the 30- and 60-minute Columbus hop additions to 1.1 oz. (31 g).

AVERY BREWING COMPANY

BOULDER, COLORADO

THOUGH THE BRAND NAME isn't always as recognizable as neighboring microbreweries such as New Belgium or Great Divide, most microbrew maniacs are familiar with one of Avery's best: the delicious Maharaja, a beautiful, hop-happy IPA with a Taj Mahallian ABV of 10 to 12 percent and consistently rated as one of the tastiest beers in the world on the websites BeerAdvocate.com and RateBeer.com.

Established in 1993 by homebrewer Adam Avery, the Avery Brewing Company produces as wide a variety of beers as one can imagine and a few hybrids that truly defy categorization. Avery prides itself on producing products that are "thoroughly American at heart, blending Old World tradition and expertise with ingenuity, creativity, and boldness." Bold is damned right. In recent years, Avery has taken home several medals from the Great American Beer Festival, including a silver in 2012 for White Rascal, a Belgian-style witbier, and a gold for the Kaiser, a bold German-style doppelbock and one of Avery's three Dictator Series beers.

Avery produces more than 8,000 barrels of beer each year, and they can be found in most states. For those closer to Boulder, it is well worth a trip to the brewery to sample some of the more limited-release concoctions. To celebrate twenty years of brewing excellence, Avery recently bottled Twenty, a XX India pale ale brewed with four types of hops, three types of dry hops, two-row barley, and honey malts, and it packs a citrus punch at 9.7 percent ABV. Keeping the good times rolling, Avery recently rebottled Ale to the Chief, a "Presidential Pale Ale" originally released on January 20, 2009, only to be rebottled and rereleased four years later for the second inauguration of President Barack Obama.

Near or far, classic or avant-garde, Avery Brewing Company continues to blaze a trail of high-quality, down-to-earth beers for those wise enough to try them.
—*Jordan Wiklund*

Spiral Jetty

Epic Brewing, Salt Lake City, Utah

Spiral Jetty is the launching point in Epic's line of IPAs. A select mix of five American-style hops dominate with overtones of citrus, resin, and pine but are balanced by an equally complex malt profile. This is the strongest of Spiral Jetty's Classic Series of beers, coming in at 6.6 percent ABV. Spiral Jetty is named after an iconic earthwork sculpture found in Utah's Great Salt Lake. —*Matthew Schaefer*

SPECIFICATIONS	OG: 1.068	FG: 1.016	ABV: 6.6%	IBU: 55	SRM: 7.5

Crush and steep in 2 gallons (7.5 L) of water at 160°F (71°C) for 30 minutes:

- 1.2 lb. (.54 kg) Carapils

Strain the grain into your brewpot and sparge with .5 gallon (2 L) of water at 160°F (71°C). Bring the water to a boil, remove from the heat, and add:

- 6 lb. (2.72 kg) Maris Otter liquid malt extract
- 2 lb. (.9 kg) light dry malt extract

Stir well until the extract is completely dissolved. Add water to bring the total volume to 3 gal. (11.3 L). Bring the wort to a rolling boil and add:

- .73 oz. (20.7 g) CTZ hop pellets (15% AA)

Boil for 30 minutes and then add:

- .4 oz. (11.34 g) Centennial hop pellets (10.5% AA)

Boil for 25 minutes and then add:

- .5 oz. (14 g) Cascade hop pellets (6% AA)
- .5 oz. (14 g) Chinook hop pellets (13% AA)

Remove from the heat and chill the wort as quickly as possible to below 80°F (27°C), using an ice bath or wort chiller. Transfer the wort to the fermenter and add cold water to bring the total volume to 5 gal. (19 L). Aerate the wort. Add yeast:

- White Labs WLP051 California Ale V

Ferment at 62°F (17°C) until final gravity is achieved. Siphon to a secondary fermenter and dry hop for 7 days with:

- .85 oz. (24 g) Centennial hop pellets (10.5% AA)
- .6 oz. (17 g) Amarillo hop pellets (9.5% AA)

Bottle when fermentation is complete with:

- 5 oz. (140 g) corn sugar

ALL-GRAIN INSTRUCTIONS

Replace the malt extract with 13 lb. (5.9 kg) of Marris Otter malt. Crush the grains and mash at 152° F (67° C) for 60 minutes. Sparge with 170°F (79°C) water to reach a total volume 6 gal. (22.7 L) in the brewpot for a 60-minute boil. Reduce the 60-minute CTZ hop addition to .63 oz. (17.86 g) and reduce the 30-minute Centennial hops addition to .23 oz. (6.5 g).

SPECIAL INSTRUCTIONS

CTZ hops are a common name signifying Columbus, Tomahawk, or Zeus hops. They all come from the same cultivar but are grown by different farms. While there will be slight flavor changes from one to another, they are generally considered interchangeable.

EPIC BREWING

SALT LAKE CITY, UTAH

WHEN THE STATE YOU LIVE IN restricts your entrepreneurial dreams, there's little to be done except live vicariously through the states around you—that's why Epic Brewing Company co-owners David Cole and Peter Erickson remember traveling to California, Oregon, and other states around Utah to sample the best of western microbrews.

When the state you live in suddenly changes the law and makes opening a brewery legal, there's only one word for it: Epic.

When Utah amended the state constitution in 2008 to make brewing possible, Cole and Erickson jumped at the chance. Channeling their business acumen acquired from years of running an international aquaculture company, the duo moved quickly to shift their focus from the water to beer. No one drank tank water—but maybe everyone would try Epic beer.

The gamble worked. Since its opening, Epic has been winning medals for a wide variety of styles at the Great American Beer Festival. In 2010, Epic took bronze for Oatmeal Stout, and in 2011 and 2012, they followed up with silver in the Fruit Beer category and a pair of bronze medals in the Herb and Spice beer and Imperial India Pale Ale categories. Teaming with brewmaster Kevin Crompton, Epic Brewing lives up to its name. With more than twenty years of professional brewing experience, Crompton is the right man to have at the helm; they even named a regular beer on tap after him—Capt'n Crompton's

Pale Ale, in the Epic Classic series. The Classic Series also includes wheat, IPA, porter, lager, and amber ales.

According to the website, the Epic team goes "all out" in everything they do. The brewery began with six fermentation tanks, allowing Crompton to mix and match styles and flavors as he saw fit. Since then (and since the medals and other award-winning concoctions), Epic has expanded its square footage and brewing capacity several times—they're even opening a taproom in Denver, scheduled to pour its first beers sometime in the fall of 2013.

Besides the six beers in the Classic Series, Epic's Elevated Series "[showcases] the variability . . . within a beer style." Every label in the Elevated Series is numbered so consumers can reference the history and details of each bottle in their hands. Recent Epic Series brews include 825 State Stout (the same 2010 GABF bronze winner), Brainless Belgian-Style, Copper Cone Pale Ale, and Hopulent IPA. More adventurous visitors to the brewery might want to try any number of beers from the Exponential Series, including Brainless on Peaches Belgian-Style Ale, Smoked & Oaked Belgian-Style Ale, Sour Apple Saison, or Fermentation Without Representation Imperial Pumpkin Porter.

"Life Elevated" is the Utah state slogan. Given the wide variety and recognition of Epic's lineup, *elevated* is an excellent way to describe its beers, its philosophy, and its future. —*Jordan Wiklund*

Thrust!

Red Eye Brewing Company, Wausau, Wisconsin

Dissatisfied with the same-old brewpub beers, Kevin Eichelberger opened Red Eye in 2008 intent on bringing different flavors to central Wisconsin. Belgians, bold IPAs, and seldom-seen styles are his strong suit, sometimes infused with unexpected flavors from ingredients like chamomile, caramelized figs, and flowers. Thrust! is one of Eichelberger's most popular brews. Loads of late-addition hops and dry hops give this strong-ish American IPA a big, fruity nose and even bigger citrusy flavor. Eichelberger notes that the acidulated malt in this recipe is used to bring his mash pH into the proper 5.2 to 5.3 range. If the water in your area is soft, you may want to consider leaving it out.

SPECIFICATIONS	OG: 1.071	FG: 1.012	ABV: 7.4%	IBU: 75	SRM: 7–9

Crush and steep these grains in .75 gal. (2.8 L) of water at 160°F (71°C) for 30 minutes:

- 6 oz. (170 g) Simpsons Crystal 10L malt
- 4 oz. (113 g) Weyermann acidulated malt
- 2 oz. (57 g) Simpsons Crystal 75L malt
- .6 oz. (17 g) Columbus hop pellets (15% AA)
- .5 oz. (14 g) Summit hop pellets (14.2% AA)

Strain the grain into your brewpot and sparge with .5 gal. (2 L) of water at 160°F (71°C). Bring the wort to a boil, remove from the heat, and add:

- 6 lb. (2.7 kg) light liquid malt extract
- .25 oz. (7 g) gypsum

Stir well until the extract is completely dissolved. Add water as needed to bring the total volume to 3 gal. (11.3 L). Bring the wort to a rolling boil. Boil for 30 minutes and then add:

- .6 oz. (17 g) Cascade hop pellets (6% AA)

Boil for 10 minutes and then add:

- .25 oz. (7 g) Columbus hop pellets (15% AA)
- .3 oz. (8.5 g) Cascade hop pellets (6% AA)

Boil for 15 minutes and then add:

- .6 oz. (17 g) Columbus hop pellets (15% AA)
- .6 oz. (17 g) Cascade hop pellets (6% AA)

Boil for 5 minutes, remove from the heat, and then add:

- .25 oz. (7 g) Cascade hop pellets (6% AA)
- .25 oz. (7 g) Columbus hop pellets (15% AA)

Chill the wort as quickly as possible to below 80°F (27°C), using an ice bath or wort chiller. Transfer the wort to the fermenter and add cold water to bring the total volume to 5 gal. (19 L). Aerate the wort. Add the yeast:

- Wyeast 1056 American Ale

Ferment at 66°F (18.9°C) until final gravity is achieved. Siphon to a secondary fermenter and add:

- 3 oz. (85 g) Cascade hop pellets (6% AA)
- .75 oz. (21 g) Chinook hop pellets (13% AA)
- .75 oz. (21 g) Columbus hop pellets (15% AA)

- .75 oz. (21 g) Willamette hop pellets (5.5% AA)
- .5 oz. (14 g) Summit hop pellets (14.2% AA)

Allow the beer to condition for no more than 5 days. Bottle when fermentation is complete with:

- 6 oz. (170 g) corn sugar

ALL-GRAIN INSTRUCTIONS

Replace the malt extract with 14.5 lb. (6.57 kg) of Rahr two-row pale malt. Crush the grains and mash at 150°F (66°C) for 60 minutes. First wort hop with .5 oz. (14 g) of Summit and .4 oz (11.3 g) Columbus hop pellets. Add .3 oz. (8.5 g) of gypsum to the mash. Sparge with 170°F (77°C) water until you reach a total volume of 6 gal. (22.7 L) in the brewpot. Reduce the 30-minute Cascade hop addition to .5 oz. (14 g). Reduce the 20-minute Cascade hop addition to .25 oz. (7 g). Reduce the 20-minute Columbus hop addition to .2 oz. (5.7 g). Reduce the 5-minute Columbus and Cascade hop additions to .5 oz. (14 g).

Watershed IPA
Oakshire Brewing, Eugene, Oregon

Oakshire Brewing in Eugene, Oregon, was launched in October 2006 by homebrewing brothers Jeff and Chris Althouse. The 15-barrel brewery has gained a regional following in the Pacific Northwest and a reputation for the brothers' innovative small-batch beers, many of which are aged in oak. They also have a reputation for community commitment, as evidenced by their Watershed IPA. One percent of revenue from Watershed IPA sales is set aside for the protection of local watersheds, as clean water is essential to their mission of brewing the highest quality beer possible. Watershed IPA has a rich, almost nutty, flavor that's well balanced by the selection of hops used in it. The Castle cara ruby malt adds to both the flavor and a beautiful reddish hue. This IPA doesn't disappoint and will have you going back for another pint.
—*Denny Conn*

Courtesy Matt Wiater (www.portlandbeer.com)

SPECIFICATIONS	OG: 1.062	FG: 1.011	ABV: 6.7%	IBU: 76	SRM: 5.7

Crush and steep these grains in 1 gal. (3.78 L) of water at 155°F (68.33°C) for 60 minutes:

- 8 oz. (225 g) Munich 10L malt
- 5 oz. (.14 kg) Castle Cara Ruby malt

Strain the grain into your brewpot and sparge with .5 gal. (2 L) of water at 160°F (71°C). Bring the wort to a boil, remove from the heat, and add:

- 6.25 lb. (2.8 kg) light dry malt extract

Note: For best results, add gypsum to bring the sulfate level of your water to 200 ppm. If you don't know your base sulfate level, add 1 rounded tsp. (5 g) of gypsum if you have soft water. Don't add gypsum if you have hard water.

Stir well until the extract is dissolved. Add water as needed to bring the volume to 3 gal. (11.3 L). Bring the wort to a rolling boil. Boil for 10 minutes, and then add:

- 1.35 oz. (38.27 g) Nugget hop pellets (13% AA)

Boil for 45 minutes, and then add:

- .25 oz. (7 g) Amarillo hop pellets (9.5% AA)
- .4 oz. (11 g) Centennial hop pellets (10.5%)
- .25 oz. (7 g) Crystal hop pellets (4.5% AA)

Boil for 15 minutes, remove from the heat, and begin chilling; then add:

- .6 oz. (17 g) Zythos hop pellets (10.9% AA)

Remove from the heat and chill as quickly as possible to below 80°F (27°C). Transfer the wort to the fermenter and add cold water to bring the total volume to 5 gal. (19 L). The temperature should be below 70°F (21°C) at this point. Aerate the wort and pitch an appropriately sized starter of:

- White Labs WLP001 California Ale or Wyeast 1056 American Ale

Ferment at 65–67°F (18–19°C) until final gravity is reached. Siphon to a secondary fermenter and add:

- 1.35 oz. (38.3 g) Amarillo hop pellets (9.5% AA)
- .5 oz. (14 g) Simcoe hop pellets (13% AA)

Allow the beer to condition for 7 days. When fermentation is complete, bottle with:

- 5 oz. (140 g) corn sugar

ALL-GRAIN INSTRUCTIONS

Replace extract with 13.25 lb. (6 kg) Great Western or Rahr two-row pale malt. Crush the grain and mash all grain at 153°F (67°C) for 60 minutes. Sparge with 170°F (77°C) water until you reach a total volume of 6 gal. (27 L) in the brewpot. Reduce the 60-minute Nugget hop addition to 1.13 oz. (32 g). Reduce the 15-minute Centennial hop addition to .34 oz. (9.64 g). Reduce the 15-minute Amarillo hop addition to .21 oz. (5.95 g). Reduce the 15-minute Crystal hop addition to .22 oz. (6.23 g). Follow recommendations above for sulfate level.

OAKSHIRE BREWING
EUGENE, OREGON

Courtesy Matt Wiater (www.portlandbeer.com)

OAKSHIRE BREWING sits a few hundred miles south of Portland, Oregon, in the city of Eugene, near the western border of Willamette National Forest. It was established in 2006 by homebrewing brothers Jeff and Chris Althouse, who attribute some of the brewery's success to the committed spirit of the people around it. Inspired and surrounded by the rugged Pacific Northwest landscape, Oakshire's motto—"Strength. Independence. Community."—evokes the brewers' devotion to their craft, as well as the benevolent spirit of the people who help make the Eugene community wonderful.

With a modest fifteen-barrel production, Oakshire's commitment to brewing fine beer runs deeper than a few words on the masthead. Indeed, the twenty-some people who work at Oakshire round-the-clock each have a profile on the website, and the brewery itself is often host to many different classes, tastings, and other nonprofit community organizations and endeavors.

The man behind some of Oakshire's success is brewmaster Matt Van Wyk, a Chicago native who brought more than ten years of fine craft-brewing experience over the Rocky Mountains to settle in the Oregon forests. Van Wyk is the proud owner of more than ten Great American Beer Festival medals, including a silver from 2009 in the Coffee Flavored Beer category with Oakshire's toasty Overcast Espresso Stout, one of the brewery's most popular regular ales. Van Wyk has also garnered two medals in the World Beer Cup awards, and it shows in every batch that Oakshire produces.

Though smaller than some of its competitors, Oakshire takes great pride in the regular, seasonal, and specialty beers available in and around the brewery. With ABVs from 5 to 9 percent, Oakshire's year-round beers include Watershed IPA ("pairs well with grilled brisket, smoked pork shoulder, spice cake, and creme brulee"); Oakshire Amber (the first beer Oakshire ever produced); and Overcast Espresso Stout (for those cold, crisp mornings near the mountains).

There's a beer for every season as well, including the wintry Ill-Tempered Gnome (a hearty winter ale); O'Dark:30, a rich, crisp springtime ale; Line Dry Ale, a mellow, citrusy summer brew; and Harvest Ale, a refreshing lager to watch the leaves turn from green to gold to yellow to red, and finally wrap up the season in time for another chilly winter (and more Oakshire beer).

Oakshire beers can be hard to find outside of the brewery's native Oregon location, but if you're ever passing through Willamette National Forest or road-tripping north to the Canadian border, stopping by the Oakshire Brewery is worth the time. You may even find some Single Batch or Brewers' Reserve on hand and a few friends to share it with. —*Jordan Wiklund*

2

PORTERS & STOUTS

When most people think of stouts they picture that pint of Guinness—the creamy off-white foam cascading into the impenetrable blackness of the underlying beer. For many that dusky hue equates to heavy. How many times have you heard someone say, "Oh, that's thick," when pouring a stout or porter?

It's time to put that myth to rest. Black is neither a flavor nor a texture. Color tells you surprisingly little about how a beer might ultimately taste. The many sub-styles of Porter and stout run the gamut from dry and light to heavy and sweet. On the lighter end is the sessionable Irish stout. That so-called "meal-in-a-glass" Guinness, for example, is under 4 percent alcohol and has only a few more calories than a typical American light lager. Intense rostiness and a creamy texture from nitrogen gas give the impression of a much fuller-bodied beer. Moving up the ladder are robust and Baltic porters as well as milk, oatmeal, and foreign "extra stouts." All feature rich chocolate and coffee flavors with varying levels of sweetness and roast. But the style reaches its pinnacle with the luscious thickness of Russian imperial stout.

What's the difference between a porter and a stout? That's hard to say. The line is blurry, and the same adjectives are used to describe both. I've come to the conclusion that a beer is a porter or a stout mostly because the brewer says it is. I believe that history bears this out.

Long ago in England, "stout" simply meant strong beer. There were pale stouts and brown stouts. Porter referred to a type of aged brown beer that was popular with the ticket porters in London. Porter came in varying strengths, with the strongest being called "stout porter."

From the mid-1700s to the late 1800s porter enjoyed immense popularity, and its production changed the way beer was made. Porter was the first mass-produced beer and one of the first mass-produced products of the industrial revolution. London's biggest porter brewers were cranking out beer in volumes that exceed most of today's regional breweries. Porter brewers initiated the practice of bulk-aging beers, keeping it in vats holding thousands of gallons. They were the first to use the thermometer and hydrometer to better control the brewing process.

At the end of the nineteenth century, the popularity of porter began to fade as tastes moved to pale ales. As alcohol levels in beer declined generally, the term "stout" became more singularly associated with strong porters. By the early twentieth century the style had nearly disappeared. Porter was so out of favor that many brewers didn't want their product associated with it. They simply called their black beers stout. It wasn't until the 1980s that American and English craft brewers began to revive the once-proud style.

Buffalo Sweat
Tallgrass Brewing Company, Manhattan, Kansas

Tallgrass Brewing Company of Manhattan, Kansas, produced its first beer in 2007. The idea was hatched a year earlier when founder Jeff Gill's wife, Tricia, asked him what he wanted to do with the rest of his life. The avid homebrewer answered that question by opening a brewery. Tallgrass beers are available in cans throughout the Midwest. One of Tallgrass' flagships, Buffalo Sweat Milk Stout, has a name that evokes the tallgrass prairies that surround Manhattan. The addition of unfermentable lactose gives this beer a creamy-smooth mouthfeel without a lot of added sweetness. It's far richer than its 5 percent alcohol would suggest. Tallgrass head brewer Andrew Hood recommends brewing the all-grain recipe for the best mouthfeel. —*Matthew Schaefer*

SPECIFICATIONS	OG: 1.057	FG: 1.020–1.024	ABV: 4.5–5%	IBU: 20	SRM: 41–42

Crush and steep these grains in 3.5 gal. (13.25 L) of water at 160°F (71°C) for 30 minutes:

- 1.2 lb. (.54 kg) Briess roasted barley
- 1.1 lb. (.49 kg) Briess Goldpils Vienna malt
- 10.5 oz. (298 g) flaked oats
- 8.8 oz. (250 g) Briess Victory malt
- 7.2 oz. (204 g) Briess Black malt

Strain the grain into your brewpot and sparge with .5 gal. (2 L) of water at 160°F (71°C). Bring the wort to a boil, remove from the heat, and add:

- 3.15 lb. (1.43 kg) light liquid malt extract
- 1.7 lb. (.77 kg) light dry malt extract
- 8 oz. (225 g) lactose

Stir well until the extract is completely dissolved. Add water as needed to bring the total volume to 3 gal. (11.3 L). Bring the wort to a rolling boil. Boil for 15 minutes and then add:

- .75 oz. (21 g) Glacier hop pellets (6% AA)

Boil for 55 minutes and then add:

- .25 oz. (7 g) Glacier hop pellets (6% AA)

Remove the wort from the heat and chill it as quickly as possible to below 80°F (27°C), using an ice bath or wort chiller. Transfer the wort to the fermenter and add cold water to bring the total volume to 5 gal. (19 L). Aerate the wort. Add the yeast:

- Wyeast 1450 Denny's Favorite

Ferment at 67°F (19°C) until final gravity is achieved. Perform a diacetyl rest by raising the temperature to 70°F (21°C) for 48 hours. Siphon to a secondary fermenter and allow the beer to condition for 5 to 7 days. Bottle when fermentation is complete with:

- 6 oz. (170 g) corn sugar

ALL-GRAIN INSTRUCTIONS

Replace the malt extract with 8.15 lb. (3.7 kg) of Briess two-row brewer's malt. Crush the grains and mash at 157°F (69°C) for 60 minutes. Raise the temperature to 170°F (77°C) and rest for 10 minutes. Sparge with 170°F (77°C) water until you reach a total volume of 6 gal. (22.7 L) in the brewpot. Reduce the 60-minute Glacier hop addition to .67 oz. (19 g). Reduce the 5-minute Glacier hop addition to .2 oz. (5.7 g).

Malpais Stout
La Cumbre Brewing Company, Albuquerque, New Mexico

Garnering a silver medal at the 2011 Great American Beer Festival, La Cumbre's Malpais Stout is a meal in a glass described as a "full onslaught of creamy stout intensity." Brewed loosely in the style of a Foreign Extra Stout, Malpais is brewed with a variety of malts, which give it a richness and intensity that is only heightened by extended boiling times.

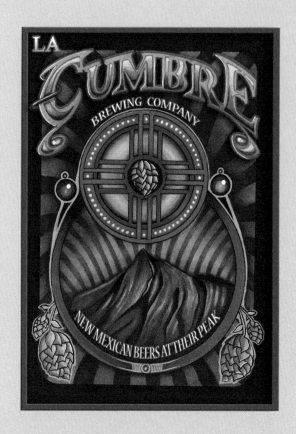

PRO BREWER'S TIP

This style of beer is a great bigger beer to brew quickly or to extract brew if you are a novice, due to the high use of roasted malts that can often temper any brewing mistakes. Often, the on-tap stout at La Cumbre is less than two weeks old. The roasted malts are fresh, big, and brash. Within a few months, the caramel begins to come through and the roasted qualities mellow.

Do not rest the mash for longer than needed to accomplish conversion unless you want a thin imperial stout. Letting it rest for 60 minutes or so could lead to a wort that attenuates to 1.014, resulting in a beer over 8.5 percent ABV.

This is a great recipe for experimenting with different brands of caramel and roasted malts. Instead of a caramel malt, why not try Gambrinus honey malt? Instead of flaked barley, why not try oats, rye, or wheat? At the end of the day, it will still be black and it will still be a foreign-style stout, so have some fun with it.

This is also a great recipe for experimenting with different yeast strains, but whichever yeast strain you use, do not let this beer sit on the yeast cake for long. Autolyzed flavors might be mitigated a bit by roasted malts, but the soy characteristic that can be picked up is truly foul. Rack to secondary or keg no more than ten days after brewing.

SPECIFICATIONS	OG: 1.080	FG: 1.025	ABV: 7.0%	IBU: 45	SRM: 60

Crush and steep in 3.5 gal. (13.25 L) of water at 160°F (71°C) for 30 minutes:

- 1 lb. (.45 kg) Crisp Extra-Dark Crystal malt
- 1 lb. (.45 kg) flaked barley
- 8 oz. (225 g) Crisp Chocolate malt
- 8 oz. (225 g) Crisp roasted barley
- 8 oz. (225 g) Franco-Belges Kiln Coffee malt

Strain the grain into your brewpot and sparge with .5 gal. (2 L) of water at 160°F (71°C). Bring the water to a boil, remove from the heat, and add:

- 6.6 lb. (3 kg) Muntons Extra-Light liquid malt extract
- 1.55 lb. (.7 kg) Muntons Extra-Light dry malt extract

Stir well until the extract is completely dissolved. Add water as needed to bring the total volume to 3 gal. (11.3 L). Bring the wort to a rolling boil and add:

- 1.12 oz. (31.75 g) UK Pilgrim hop pellets (10.5% AA)

Boil for 90 minutes. Remove from the heat and chill the wort as quickly as possible to below 80°F (27°C), using an ice bath or wort chiller. Transfer the wort to the fermenter and add cold water to bring the total volume to 5 gal. (19 L). Aerate the wort. Add the yeast:

- Wyeast 1056 American Ale, White Labs WLP001 California Ale, or Safale US-05

Ferment at 62°F (17°C) until final gravity is achieved. Siphon to a secondary fermenter, and allow the beer to condition for 7 to 10 days. Bottle when fermentation is complete with:

- 5 oz. (140 g) corn sugar

ALL-GRAIN INSTRUCTIONS

Replace the base malt extract with 13.25 lb. (6 kg) of Crisp pale malt. Mash at 150°F (66°C) for 60 minutes. Sparge with 170°F (77°C) water until you reach a total volume of 7.5 gal. (28.4 L) in the brewpot. Boil for 150 minutes. Reduce the 90-minute UK Pilgrim Hop addition to .9 oz. (25.5 g).

Troy Paff, The Journeyman Project (www.journeymanproject.net)

Smoke
Surly Brewing Company, Minneapolis, Minnesota

The big-bottle, specialty releases are among the most sought-after brews from Minnesota's Surly Brewing Company. Smoke is an early-winter offering that makes a great sipper as the nights grow longer. This ebony-black and silky-smooth Baltic porter gets an aromatic boost from generous use of German smoked malt. Dark malt flavors meld with notes of raisins, plums, and licorice to create a beautifully complex sipper. Note that this recipe must be made as either partial-mash or all-grain. It is also fermented with lager yeast, so the ability to carefully control fermentation temperature is required to achieve proper results.

Adam Turman (www.adamturman.com)

SPECIFICATIONS	OG: 1.087	FG: 1.025	ABV: 8.3%	IBU: 50	SRM: 45

Heat 2.5 gal. (9.5 L) of water to 163°F (73°C). Crush and add the following specialty grains in a nylon mesh bag. Temperature should be within a degree or two of 148°F (64°C). Maintain that temperature and steep for 60 minutes:

- 5 lb. (2.25 kg) Weyermann Smoked malt
- 12 oz. (340 g) Belgian aromatic malt
- 8 oz. (225 g) English black malt
- 8 oz. (225 g) Weyermann Carafa II
- 4 oz. (113 g) English chocolate malt

While the mash rests heat 1.5 (5.7 L) gal. of water to 168°F (76°C) in a separate pot. When the mash is finished, return the pot to the heat and slowly raise the temperature to 168°F (76°C). Strain the grain into your brewpot and sparge with the water from the second pot. Bring the wort to a boil, remove from the heat, and add:

- 3.15 lb. (1.43 kg) light liquid malt extract
- 3.5 lb. (1.58 kg) light dry malt extract

Stir well until the extract is completely dissolved. Add water as needed to bring the total volume to 4 gal. (15.4 L). Bring the wort to a rolling boil, and add:

- .85 oz. (24.9 g) Warrior hop pellets (16% AA)

Boil for 60 minutes, and then chill the wort as quickly as possible to 58°F (14°C), using an ice bath or wort chiller. Transfer the wort to the fermenter, and add cold water to bring the total volume to 5 gal. (19 L). Aerate the wort. Add the yeast:

- Wyeast 2124 Bohemian Lager

Ferment at 51°F (11°C) until final gravity is achieved. Perform a diacetyl rest by raising the temperature to 65°F (18°C) for 5 days. Siphon to a secondary fermenter, and slowly lower the temperature to 33°F (1°C). After 3 weeks, add:

- 2 oz. (57 g) oak cubes (sanitize by steaming for 10 minutes or soaking in a neutral spirit)

Allow the beer to condition for 5 weeks. Bottle when fermentation is complete with:

- 5 oz. (140 g) corn sugar

ALL-GRAIN INSTRUCTIONS

Replace the malt extract with 10 lb. (4.5 kg) Canada Malting Pale Ale malt. Increase the amount of Weyermann smoked malt to 6.75 lb. (3 kg). Crush the grains and mash at 148°F (64°C) for 60 minutes. Sparge with 168°F (76°C) water until you reach a total volume of 6 gal. (22.7 L) in the brewpot. Reduce the 60-minute Warrior hop addition to .75 oz. (21 g).

Adam Turman (www.adamturman.com)

SURLY BREWING COMPANY

MINNEAPOLIS, MINNESOTA

SINCE IT OPENED IN 2006, the Surly Brewing Company has made quite a sud-soaked splash in the Twin Cities of Minnesota. Today, Surly continues to brew and distribute high-quality beer in cans and on tap all around Minnesota and the greater Midwest and has even played a critical role in changing the liquor laws of Minnesota.

But before all that, Surly was the dream of collegiate homebrewer Omar Ansari, a hop-happy brewer who'd been concocting a wide variety of tongue-tingling libations since 1994. Once Ansari decided it was brewing or bust, he apprenticed at New Holland Brewing Company in Michigan, and later enlisted Todd Haug of Rock Bottom Brewery (Minneapolis) to help set up the company, and Surly poured its first beers soon after.

Since then, the popularity of Surly has grown. Fueled by a love of community, aggressive marketing, and a bold approach to flavor and style, Surly is now one of the most recognized beer brands in the Midwest.

Part of that notoriety came from a committed group of beer drinkers who wanted, well, more beer.

Early in 2011, Surly announced its intentions of opening a beer garden and restaurant on its grounds and increasing its brewing capacity to 100,000 barrels. Minnesota's convoluted liquor laws, however, prevented that from happening. But Surly Nation (Surly's not-so-silent majority of devoted consumers) did not relent, and several members of the Minnesota Legislature were moved to amend the law, which would allow breweries to distribute and sell their beer on brewery premises. The amendment—loosely regarded as the "Surly Bill"—passed and was signed into law by Governor Mark Dayton on May 25, 2011. Plans for the new pub are in order, and it could open as soon as 2014.

Furious, Bender, CynicAle, Darkness, Smoke, and Abrasive—Surly's beers are as bold as they sound. Featuring a bevy of traditional, seasonal, and specialty brews, Surly has made its name on these tasty beers. Furious, the flagship brew, is made with "a dazzling blend of American hops and Scottish malt . . . with waves of citrus, pine, and caramel-toffee." Darkness is one of Surly's most popular seasonal brews, featuring decadent flavors that delight the devil inside the palate: chocolate, cherries, raisins, coffee, toffee, and hops. But you had better get to the liquor store or brewery early; this Russian imperial stout sells quickly. No matter how you choose to be Surly, prepare yourself: It's rare for any of Surly's beers to rate beneath 5 percent ABV. Each 16-ounce can packs a wallop.

With bold flavor, a passionate fandom, and a commitment to brewing damn good beer, Surly's future looks bright and proves once more why Minnesota should be regarded as much more than just "flyover country." —*Jordan Wiklund*

Snowstorm 2009 Baltic Porter
August Schell Brewing Company, New Ulm, Minnesota

Snowstorm is the August Schell Brewing Company's annual holiday-season special release. It's brewed to a different style every year, leading beer drinkers across the state of Minnesota to eagerly anticipate each new version. Some of the Snowstorm brews have become such fan favorites that they are now part of the brewery's regular lineup. The 2009 Baltic Porter was particularly popular, garnering several votes in my poll of homebrewers about what recipes they would like to see in this book. It's on the low end of the scale in terms of strength, but that doesn't mean the flavor is lacking. Notes of cocoa, molasses, and brown sugar carry through from sniff to swallow.

SPECIFICATIONS	OG: 1.072	FG: 1.027	ABV: 6%	IBU: 31	SRM: 29

Crush and steep these grains in 2 gal. (7.5 L) of water at 160°F (71°C) for 30 minutes:

- 8 oz. (225 g) chocolate malt
- 6.5 oz. (184 g) Victory malt
- 6 oz. (170 g) Briess Extra Special malt
- 3.5 oz. (99 g) Crystal 20L malt
- 3.5 oz. (99 g) Crystal 60L malt
- 2.5 oz. (71 g) Crystal 120L malt

Strain the grain into your brewpot and sparge with .5 gal. (2 L) of 160°F (71°C). Bring to a boil, remove from the heat, and add:

- 12 lb. (5.4 kg) Munich liquid malt extract
- 12 oz. (340 g) light dry malt extract

Stir well until the extract is completely dissolved. Add water to bring the total volume to 3 gal. (11.3 L). Bring the wort to a rolling boil, and add:

- .85 oz. (24 g) Tettnang hop pellets (4.5% AA)
- 1 oz. (28 g) Liberty hop pellets (4% AA)

Boil for 40 minutes and then add:

- .55 oz. (15.6 g) Tettnang hop pellets (4.5% AA)

Boil for 20 more minutes. Remove from the heat and chill the wort as quickly as possible to below 80°F (27°C), using an ice bath or wort chiller. Transfer the wort to the fermenter and add cold water to bring the total volume to 5 gal. (19 L). Aerate the wort. Add the yeast:

- Wyeast 2000 Budvar Lager

Ferment at 50°F (10°C) until final gravity is achieved. Siphon to a secondary fermenter and allow the beer to condition for 5 weeks at 33°F (1°C). Bottle when fermentation is complete with:

- 6 oz. (170 g) corn sugar

ALL-GRAIN INSTRUCTIONS

Replace the malt extract with 13 lb. (5.9 kg) of Munich malt. Crush the grains and mash at 147°F (64°C) for 15 minutes. Raise the temperature to 167°F (75°C) and rest for 20 minutes. Raise the temperature to 170°F (79°C). Sparge with 170°F (79°C) water until you reach a total volume of 6 gal. (22.7 L) in the brewpot. Reduce the 60-minute Tettnang hop addition to .7 oz. (20 g). Reduce the 60-minute Liberty hop addition to .8 oz. (23 g). Reduce the 20-minute Tettnang hop addition to .45 oz. (13 g).

AUGUST SCHELL BREWING COMPANY

NEW ULM, MINNESOTA

AUGUST SCHELL WAS BORN IN 1828 in Durbach, Germany, in the Black Forest region. At twenty years old, Schell left Germany for the United States, making his way north from New Orleans to Cincinnati, and later, with his wife and daughters, to Minnesota as part of the Cincinnati Turner Society, a group of northbound German immigrants. When they merged with another group of Germans, the southern Minnesota prairie town of New Ulm was born.

Schell immediately recognized Minnesota's lack of good German lager. He soon erected a small brewing company with partner Jacob Bernhardt, and the legend grew from there. Schell lived a good life, and upon his death at the age of sixty-three, the brewing company passed down to his sons. Over the next several decades, the August Schell Brewing Company changed hands several times, and though the owners' names haven't ended in Schell in more than 100 years, the Marti family is related through marriage to August.

Prohibition shut down more than 1,500 breweries around the country, and only about 600 remained to reopen after repeal. Schell's was one of them, and though times had been tough, the Marti family had recognized the value of nonalcoholic drinks as well, and now Schell's 1919 Classic American Draft Root Beer is almost as famous as the beer brand itself.

Today, the brewery counts more than thirty beers to its name, including Grain Belt, which Schell's bought in 2002 to save another legendary Minnesota beer from disappearing. Schell's remains the largest and oldest brewery in Minnesota, and as its 150th anniversary approaches, the future is bright for this historic brand.

Schell's bottles and distributes more than a dozen year-round and seasonal original and craft beers, as well as three Grain Belt–brand styles (Premium, Premium Light, and Nordeast). But it's one of the first beers of Schell's late 20th-century revival that really turned heads—the Pils.

Schell's Pils was first brewed in 1984 under the watchful (and successful) eye of owner Warren Marti. Brewed with 100 percent barley malt, the full hop flavor prompted the late, great Michael Jackson (beer connoisseur and writer, not the pop artist) to remark that Schell's Pils is "one of the best American examples of the Pilsner style." Schell's cites Pils as boasting a "rich malt body, accented by a large hop/malt aroma, and a refreshing hop tang."

Pils has many accolades to its name, including a bronze in the 1987 Great American Beer Festival Pilsner category, a gold just one year later in 1988, first place in the Domestic Premium category of the 1991 Great International Beer Tasting Festival, and more recently, a silver in 2006, again in the Great American festival. —*Jordan Wiklund*

3 WHEAT & RYE BEERS

Wheat beers . . . tart, refreshing, the perfect beers of summer. As one of mankind's oldest cultivated grains, it is almost certain that the earliest beers contained wheat. In modern times this ancient grain has spawned diverse traditions and distinct styles that are particular to different regions of the globe. In Belgium there is the ultra-light citrus and spice of witbier. Orange peel and coriander give this style a subtle floral/fruity kick. Southern Germany has the banana- and clove-tinged hefeweizen. Suspended yeast and wheat proteins make these light-bodied beers mouth-filling treats. In Berlin, brewers conjured the spritzy and slightly sour Berliner weisse, often consumed in cafés with a shot of raspberry or woodruff syrup. And in the United States there are the cleaner and more assertively hopped American wheat beer and the high-alcohol wheat wine.

And while we're at it, let's not forget wheat beer's close cousins, the equally refreshing brews made with rye. Whether malted or unmalted, rye gives beer a spicy edge that complements hops or the clove phenolics of German wheat beer yeasts.

Cloudy or clear, with fruit or straight, you really can't go wrong with the unique flavors of traditional wheat and rye beers.

But American brewers are taking these old grains in new directions that are reflected in the recipes that follow. Rye IPAs (or RyePAs) like Shmaltz's Bittersweet Lenny's RIPA play the grainy spice against the citrusy zip of hops. Lagunitas' Little Sumpin' Sumpin' is an IPA with a wheaty twist. The Bruery's Rugbrød saison is like rye bread in a glass. Wiley's Rye Ale from Wisconsin's Stone Cellar Brewpub is a smooth and sessionable American rye ale.

Rye beers used to be out of reach for extract brewers. Rye has to be put through a mash. But the introduction of rye extracts has changed all that. For all-grain brewers who have never brewed with wheat or rye, a word of caution is in order. Both grains are loaded with proteins and lack a husk that normally forms a filter while lautering barley-based beers. These proteins can gum up and form a lauter-proof block that results in a slow or stuck mash. A protein rest and the use of rice hulls are advised.

Bittersweet Lenny's R.I.P.A
Shmaltz Brewing, Clifton Park, New York

Shmaltz Brewing also brews under the He'Brew banner under which they brew the "Chosen Beers," a lineup of extreme beers. Included in that lineup is Bittersweet Lenny's R.I.P.A, a rye-based double IPA. Coming in at an astounding original gravity of 1.096 and 10 percent ABV, R.I.P.A not only provides a wonderfully complex hop profile (weaving in no less than seven different hops!), it has a malt backbone to support them. Such a complex beer cannot be brewed with extract alone, and accordingly you will need to perform at least a partial mash. That said, your hard work will be rewarded. —*Matthew Schaefer*

LICreate (www.istockphoto.com)

SPECIFICATIONS	OG: 1.096	FG: 1.010	ABV: 10%	IBU: 95–100	SRM: 8.2

Crush and steep in 2 gal. (7.57 L) of water at 155°F (68°C) in order to reach a mash temperature of 144°F (62°C):

- 4 lb. (1.8 kg) two-row malt
- 1.9 lb. (.86 kg) rye malt
- 9 oz. (255 g) flaked rye
- 4.6 oz. (130 g) wheat malt

Rest for 45 minutes and apply heat to slowly raise the temperature to 152°F (67°C). Rest for 15 minutes.

Strain the grain into your brewpot and sparge with 3 gal. (11.35 L) of water at 168°F (76°C). Add water as needed to bring the total volume to 4.25 gal. (16.1 16 L). Bring the water to a boil, remove from the heat, and add:

- 9.15 lb. (4.15 kg) pilsner liquid extract

Stir well until the extract is completely dissolved. Add water as needed to bring the total volume to 4.25 gal. (16 L). Bring to a boil, and add:

- 1.1 oz. (31 g) Warrior hop pellets (16% AA)

Boil for 40 minutes, then add:

- .45 oz. (13 g) Cascade hop pellets (6% AA)
- .45 oz. (13 g) Simcoe hop pellets (13% AA)
- .45 oz. (13 g) Warrior hop pellets (16% AA)

Boil for 10 minutes, then add:

- .45 oz. (13 g) Cascade hop pellets (6% AA)
- .45 oz. (13 g) Chinook hop pellets (13% AA)
- .45 oz. (13 g) Crystal hop pellets (4.5% AA)

Boil for 5 minutes, add:

- .3 oz. (8.5 g) Amarillo hop pellets (9.5% AA)
- .3 oz. (8.5 g) Cascade hop pellets (6% AA)
- .3 oz. (8.5 g) Simcoe hop pellets (13% AA)
- .14 oz. (4 g) ground caraway seeds

Boil for 5 more minutes and remove from the heat. Add:

- .56 oz. (16 g) Centennial hop pellets (10.5% AA)

Chill the wort as quickly as possible to below 80°F (27°C), using an ice bath or wort chiller. Transfer the wort to the fermenter and add cold water to bring the total volume to 5 gal. (19 L). Aerate the wort. Add the yeast:

- Wyeast 1056 American Ale, White Labs WLP001 California Ale, or Safale US-05

Ferment at 62°F (17°C) until final gravity is achieved. Siphon to a secondary fermenter and add:

- 1 oz. (28 g) Amarillo hop pellets (9.5% AA)

Allow the beer to condition on the dry hops for 7 days. Bottle when fermentation is complete with:

- 5 oz. (140 g) corn sugar

ALL-GRAIN INSTRUCTIONS

Replace the grain bill above with the following and mash at 144°F (62°C) for 45 minutes.

- 16.75 lb. (7.7 kg) two-row malt
- 2.25 lb. (1 kg) rye malt
- 11 oz. (312 g) flaked rye
- 5.5 oz. (156 g) wheat malt
- 4 oz. (113 g) amber malt
- 2.7 oz. (77 g) Caramunich malt
- 1.3 oz. (37 g) Crystal rye
- 1.3 oz. (37 g) Crystal 60L malt

Slowly raise the temperature to 152°F (67°C) and rest for 15 minutes. Sparge with 170°F (79°C) water until you reach a total volume of 6 gal. (22.7 L) in the brewpot. Reduce the 60-minute Warrior hop addition to .97 oz. (27.5 g).

SHMALTZ BREWING
CLIFTON PARK, NEW YORK

Dave Zalumbowski (AP Images)

L'HAIM!

For Gentile readers, *l'haim* is a traditional Jewish toast that means "to life." If there's one thing Shmaltz does well, it's celebrating its own good fortune and rejoicing in quality beer. Shmaltz was founded as "American Jewish Celebration Beer" and began, like many craft breweries, as an experiment. In 1996 during Chanukah, Jeremy Cowan and some friends decided to explore the world of home brewing and mixed one of their first batches with hand-squeezed pomegranate juice. They called it "He'Brew Beer" and delivered it around the San Francisco Bay Area in Cowan's grandmother's beat-up Volvo.

Thus began the legend of He'Brew Beer and the Shmaltz Brewing Company. In 1997, Anderson Valley Brewing Company (Boonville, California) began distributing He'Brew Beer to wholesalers, and Cowan began his tenure as a full-time brewer. By 2003, Cowan found himself in New York, brewing and distributing beer through the Mendocino Brewing Company in Saratoga Springs. There are now six regular beers included in the He'Brew series: Origin Pomegranate Strong Ale, Messiah Bold, Bittersweet Lenny's R.I.P.A., Genesis Ale, Jewbelation, and Rejewvenator.

In 2008, Shmaltz grew again with the launch of the Coney Island Craft Lagers series of beers. Partnering with Coney Island USA—a certified 501(c)(3) nonprofit organization—a small portion of every sale from the Coney Island line goes back to the nonprofit. The line is headed by Coney Island Lager and features five other experimental lagers, including three regular lagers and two seasonals.

The Shmaltz Brewing Company is not shy about its products or its heritage. Every line and bottle features striking artwork and imagery related to the faith-inspired names of its products, and the company is widely recognized for its tongue-in-cheek yet serious examination of the Jewish world and history and its intersection with popular pop culture. For example, the tagline for Messiah Bold lager is "the beer you've been waiting for," alluding to the Jewish belief that the Messiah is yet to come. Bittersweet Lenny's R.I.P.A. is a tribute and homage to late comedian Lenny Bruce, and the beer is brewed with an "obscene" amount of hops. In 2010, the barrel-aged edition of R.I.P.A. garnered the silver medal in the Wood- and Barrel-Aged Strong Beer category at the Great American Beer Festival.

He'Brew Beers and Coney Island Craft Lagers can be found in over thirty states around the nation, both in liquor stores and directly from wholesalers. True believers in the company will want to make a pilgrimage to New York, however, to experience the full pantheon of Shmaltz's many offerings, seeking the grace and retribution that comes with a good beer after a long journey. Shmaltz brews many limited-edition styles and flavors of its products, many inspired by and brewed within the Jewish adherence to numerology in its batches—in 2011, the fifteenth anniversary of Shmaltz merited 15:15 Genesis barleywine, brewed with 15 varieties of malts and hops, delivering a whopping 15 percent ABV libation!

If there's one thing beer drinkers can all agree on, it's good beer from fine companies. No matter your background or what you believe, Schmaltz has something for you. —*Jordan Wiklund*

Little Sumpin' Sumpin' Ale
Lagunitas Brewing Company, Petaluma, California

With a reputation for irreverence, Lagunitas Brewing Company isn't afraid to mess with the classic styles. In fact, that's the company's stock-in-trade. So what sort of transgression can Lagunitas cook up for India pale ale, perhaps the most over-done style on the planet? Load it down with extra hops? Been there, done that. How about wheat? A grist bill of 50 percent wheat malt—three different kinds—gives Little Sumpin' Sumpin' a light golden color and hazy complexion. Oh, and it's still loaded with hops.

SPECIFICATIONS	OG: 1.070	FG: 1.013	ABV: 7.5%	IBU: 34.7	SRM: 4–5

Crush and steep the following in 2 gal. (7.5 L) of water at 160°F (71°C) for 30 minutes:

- 1.6 lb. (.73 kg) unmalted wheat
- 3 oz. (85 g) Dingemans Roasted Wheat malt

Strain the grain into your brewpot and sparge with .5 gal. (2 L) of water at 160°F (71°C). Bring the wort to a boil, remove from the heat, and add:

- 6 lb. (2.7 kg) wheat liquid malt extract
- 2 lb. (.9 kg) light dry malt extract

Stir well until the extract is completely dissolved. Add water as needed to bring the total volume to 3 gal. (11.3 L). Bring the wort to a rolling boil and add:

- .2 oz. (5.67 g) Nugget hop pellets (13% AA)
- .1 oz. (3 g) Horizon hop pellets (12% AA)
- .1 oz. (3 g) Summit hop pellets (14.2% AA)

Boil for 45 minutes and then add:

- .3 oz. (9 g) Willamette hop pellets (5.5% AA)

Boil for 30 minutes and then add:

- 1 oz. (28 g) Santiam hop pellets (6.5% AA)
- .3 oz. (9 g) Willamette hop pellets (5.5% AA)

Boil for 15 minutes. Remove from the heat. Chill the wort as quickly as possible to below 80°F (27°C), using an ice bath or wort chiller. Transfer the wort to the fermenter and add cold water to bring the total volume to 5 gal. (19 L). Aerate the wort. Add the yeast:

- WLP002 English Ale

Ferment at 62–65°F (17–18°C) for 36 hours. Raise the temperature to 68°F (20°C) and rest for 36 hours. Raise the temperature to 70°F (21°C) and hold until final gravity is achieved. Siphon to a secondary fermenter and add:

- .7 oz. (20 g) Cascade hop pellets (6% AA)
- .7 oz. (20 g) Centennial hop pellets (10.5% AA)
- .7 oz. (20 g) Chinook hop pellets (13% AA)
- .7 oz. (20 g) Simcoe hop pellets (13% AA)

- .5 oz. (14 g) Amarillo hop pellets (9.5% AA)
- .45 oz. (13 g) Columbus hop pellets (15% AA)

Allow the beer to condition for 5 to 7 days. Bottle when fermentation is complete with:

- 6 oz. (170 g) corn sugar

ALL-GRAIN INSTRUCTIONS

Replace the malt extract with 7.3 lb. (3.3 kg) of two-row pale malt and 5.5 lb. (2.5 kg) of wheat malt. Crush the grains and mash at 150°F (66°C) for 60 minutes. Sparge with 170°F (77°C) water until you reach a total volume of 6.5 gal. (24.6 L) in the brewpot. Reduce the 90-minute Nugget hop addition to .2 oz. (5.67 g). Reduce the 90-minute Horizon and Summit hop additions to .06 oz. (1.7 g). Reduce the 45-minute Willamette hop addition to .2 oz. (6 g). Reduce the 15-minute Santiam hop addition to .8 oz. (23 g). Reduce the 15-minute Willamette hop addition to .3 oz. (9 g).

Rugbrød
The Bruery, Placentia, California

"Rugbrød" is Danish for "rye bread." That dark and earthy Scandinavian staple provided the inspiration for this dark brown beer, which is loosely based on the traditional Scandinavian Christmas beer "Julebryg." Three types of rye give it an earthy, spicy bite that is enhanced by just a hint of roast. Add a side of bready, nutty barley malt and Belgian yeast, and you've got a festive brew that's appropriate for any time of year.

SPECIFICATIONS		OG: 1.070	FG: 1.008	ABV: 8%	IBU: 30	SRM: 27

Crush and steep in 2.5 gal. (9.5 L) of water at 160°F (71°C) for 30 minutes:

- 1.06 lb. (.48 kg) Great Western caramel 60 malt
- 9.6 oz. (272 g) Bairds Brown malt
- 9.6 oz. (272 g) Simpsons Crystal Rye malt
- 4.8 oz. (136 g) chocolate rye malt

Strain the grain into your brewpot and sparge with .5 gal. (2 L) of water at 160°F (71°C). Bring the wort to a boil, remove from the heat, and add:

- 8.5 lb. (3.85 kg) rye liquid malt extract

Stir well until the extract is completely dissolved. Add water as needed to bring the total volume to 3 gal. (11.3 L). Bring the wort to a rolling boil and add:

- .5 oz. (14 g) Warrior hop pellets (16% AA)

Boil for 60 minutes and then remove from the heat. Chill the wort as quickly as possible to below 80°F (27°C), using an ice bath or wort chiller. Transfer the wort to the fermenter and add cold water to bring the total volume to 5 gal. (19 L). Aerate the wort. Add the yeast:

- WLP570 Belgian Golden Ale

Ferment at 74°F (18°C) until final gravity is achieved. Siphon to a secondary fermenter and allow the beer to condition for 5 to 7 days. Bottle when fermentation is complete with:

- 6 oz. (170 g) corn sugar

ALL-GRAIN INSTRUCTIONS

Replace malt extract with 9.5 lb. (4.3 kg) Great Western two-row pale malt and 3.6 lb. (1.6 kg) Weyermann rye malt. Crush the grains and mash at 155°F (68°C) for 60 minutes. Sparge with 170°F (77°C) water until you reach a total volume of 6 gal. (22.7 L) in the brewpot. Reduce the Warrior hop addition to .45 oz. (13 g).

THE BRUERY
PLACENTIA, CALIFORNIA

SINCE IT OPENED IN 2006, the Bruery of Orange County, California, has turned heads and tempted palates of adventurous bastions of beer far and wide. Formed by brothers Patrick and Chris Rue, the Bruery—a portmanteau of the word *brewery* and the name *Rue*—has garnered quite a reputation for its nontraditional beer flavors and old-world brewing methods. What began as a diversion from law school for Patrick grew into an obsession and finally blossomed into a business for the brothers Rue.

Many of the beers are brewed in the Belgian tradition, meaning none of them are filtered or pasteurized. Most of the carbonation in the bottled beers derives from bottle conditioning and a secondary bottle fermentation process. The Bruery prides itself on crafting "complex flavors from simple ingredients" and is devoted to creating wholesome beers in wholesome ways.

One of the goals of the Bruery is to push the limits of what beer really *is.* First, its quaffs are *strong*—their bourbon-aged ales often range from 13 to 19 percent ABV. If that sounds a lot like wine, it's because, well, those flavors and styles are incorporated into the beer. The Vitis series blends syrah, chardonnay, and pinots into its concoctions. The Orchard White, for example, sounds a lot more like a wine than a beer. In the bottle, Orchard White is an unfiltered, bottle-conditioned Belgian-style witbier, golden in color and spiced with citrus peel,

lavender, coriander, and more, and a fruity, yeasty strain adds complexity and subtle flavors to the end product. In 2008, *Draft* magazine named it one of the top 25 beers of the year, while *Beer Advocate Magazine* rated it a solid "A."

The Bruery produces about 2,500 barrels of beer annually, which can be found in many parts of the United States, including southern California, the Pacific Northwest, many Midwest states, the upper East Coast, and Florida. The Bruery produces six beers year round: Saison Rue, a Belgian-style ale brewed with rye; Mischief, a hoppy Belgian-style golden; Loakal Red, an oak-aged American red ale; Humulus Lager, a strong Imperial Pale Lager; Rugbrød, a Danish-style rye; and Hottenroth, a German-style wheat beer. Many other seasonal and brewery-only special batches are available, and a comprehensive map of where to find their brews can be found on the Bruery's website.

If you don't find something nearby, don't fret; that time is rapidly approaching. Since 2010, the Bruery has taken home medals every year in the Great American Beer Festival, including gold medals in 2010 for Oude Tart in the Belgian-style sour category and in 2011 for Papier in the Strong Ale category. No matter how and when you try it, the Bruery will challenge your modern conception of what good beer can—and possibly should—truly be.
—*Jordan Wiklund*

Wiley's Rye Ale
Stone Cellar Brewpub, Appleton, Wisconsin

A visit to the Stone Cellar Brewpub provides a literal connection to the history of brewing in Wisconsin. The 1859 building originally housed the Appleton Brewing and Malting Company. The pub's dining room and bar are located in the former lagering cellars. Two Stone Cellar beers, Pilsner and Adler Brau, are taken from the old brewery's recipe archives. Not historic, but nonetheless interesting, Wiley's Rye Ale exhibits a solid balance of hop bitterness and flavor, combined with the strong fruity flavors contributed by the liberal use of rye malt in the grain bill. Brewmaster Steve Lonsway recommends adding a bit of gypsum if your area has soft water.

SPECIFICATIONS	OG: 1.058	FG: 1.013	ABV: 6%	IBU: 24	SRM: 12–13

Crush and steep in 3 gal. (11.3 L) of water at 160°F (71°C) for 30 minutes:

- 1.2 lb. (.54 kg) Briess flaked rye
- 1.2 lb. (.54 kg) Briess Munich 10L malt
- .8 lb. (.36 kg) Briess Caramel 80L malt

Strain the grain into your brewpot and sparge with .5 gal. (2 L) of water at 160°F (71°C). Bring the wort to a boil, remove from the heat, and add:

- 6 lb. (2.7 kg) rye liquid malt extract

Stir well until the extract is completely dissolved. Add water as needed to bring the total volume to 3 gal. (11.3 L). Bring the wort to a rolling boil and add:

- .35 oz. (10 g) Nugget hop pellets (13% AA)

Boil for 60 minutes and then add:

- .5 oz. (14 g) Challenger hop pellets (6.5% AA)

Boil for 15 minutes, remove from the heat, and then add:

- .3 oz. (9 g) Challenger hop pellets (6.5% AA)

Chill the wort as quickly as possible to below 80°F (27°C), using an ice bath or wort chiller. Transfer the wort to the fermenter and add cold water to bring the total volume to 5 gal. (19 L). Aerate the wort. Add the yeast:

- Wyeast 1318 London Ale III, WLP013 London Ale, or Danstar Nottingham Ale

Ferment at 65°F (18°C) until final gravity is achieved. Siphon to a secondary fermenter and add:

- .42 oz. (11.9 g) Willamette whole-leaf hops (5.5% AA)

Allow the beer to condition for five to seven days. Bottle when fermentation is complete with:

- 6 oz. (170 g) corn sugar

ALL-GRAIN INSTRUCTIONS

Replace malt extract with 6.35 lb. (2.9 kg) of Briess two-row brewer's malt and 2.77 lb. (1.25 kg) of Briess rye malt. Increase Briess flaked rye to 1.38 lb. (.62 kg). Increase Briess Munich 10L malt to 1.38 lb. (.62 kg). Increase Briess 80L Caramel malt to .92 lb. (.41 kg). Crush the grains and mash with .25 lb. (.11 kg) of rice hulls at 152°F (67°C) for 60 minutes. Sparge with 170°F (77°C) water until you reach a total volume of 6.25 gal. (23.7 L) in the brewpot. Reduce the 75-minute Nugget hop addition to .33 oz. (9.35 g). Reduce the 15-minute Challenger hop addition to .42 oz. (11.9 g).

STONE CELLAR BREWPUB
APPLETON, WISCONSIN

FROM THE ROLLING FIELDS OF WISCONSIN and the pastoral town of Appleton comes the Stone Cellar Brewpub. With a recent expansion that includes a beer garden and taproom, Stone Cellar's brewers have been practicing their trade for more than 150 years.

Stone Cellar's story began in 1858 with a German immigrant named Anton Fischer. During that time, "Yankee Progressivism" was bumping heads with the stalwart Puritans of the area. The production, sale, and quaffing of alcoholic beverages was strictly *verboten*, but Fischer didn't care. He opened a brewery anyway.

In 1860, he sold the building to Carl Muench, an ambitious young gentleman with experience from the nearby Joseph Schlitz Brewing Company in Milwaukee (or "The Good Land," as some Wisconsin beer drinkers may know). Fast-forward a few decades, and the business was later sold to the Walter Brewery Company. Doors were closed during Prohibition but reopened to much acclaim by George Walter near the end of the Roaring Twenties, and the beer flowed freely, including a much-loved light, mild lager called Adler Brau (German for "eagle beer"). The high-flying brew remained one of the most popular in the area for generations.

In 1974, however, unable to compete with larger breweries and national distributors, Walter Brewery closed its doors and wouldn't reopen until 1989, when new ownership dubbed it the Adler Brau Brewery and Restaurant, later changing the name to Stone Cellar Brewpub.

Times changed again, and in 2009, Stone Cellar Brewpub began to focus on sustainability, pledging to remain as eco-friendly as possible by sourcing local products and devoting itself to reducing any extra waste and energy consumption. Now, Stone Cellar provides beer to more than one hundred regional restaurants and bars and continues to foster local relationships with green-friendly businesses and nonprofits.

Though you may have to travel to get it, Stone Cellar brews an array of ales, lagers, pilsners, and more. The Houdini Honey Wheat is brewed with pure Wisconsin honey. Specialty brews are also available year round, including a dopplebock and barley wine in the spring, blueberry wheat and raspberry porters in the summer, pumpkin spice in the fall, and toasty winter ales during colder months.

As of 2013, the future of Stone Cellar Brewpub isn't set in beer-soaked stone quite yet. Stone Cellar plans to continue doing what it does best, however: remaining local, thinking regionally, and producing low-waste, high-quality, delicious Wisconsin beer.
—*Jordan Wiklund*

4 BELGIANS

Belgium has evolved one of the most unique brewing cultures in the world. Unfettered by silly restrictions, like the German *Reinheitsgebot* or purity law that restricted brewers to barley, hops, water, and yeast, Belgian brewers have been free to explore nontraditional ingredients like fruits, spices, and sugars. But what really identifies a "Belgian" beer is the yeast. The delectable combinations of fruity and spicy flavors brought by Belgian yeast strains are unmistakable and yet difficult to verbalize. Lacking better language, I call it "cotton candy."

But yeast isn't the only thing that defines Belgian beer. Subtlety, balance, and drinkability are also keys. No one element should overwhelm. Spices, fruits, and other adjuncts should be kept just at the edge of perception. The goal is a delicate dance of flavors that delivers layers of complexity from relatively simple recipes. But be careful. High alcohol is another characteristic of the Belgian ales. These high-test brews go down dangerously easily.

The range of Belgian styles is enormous, though Belgian brewers tend to eschew the notion of "style" altogether. There are the abbey styles, including tripels, dubels, and singles. Those bearing the designation "Trappist ale" are still brewed by monks at one of eight Trappist monasteries. Then there are blonde ales, strong golden and strong dark ales, and quadruples, not to mention the traditional farmhouse ales, saison and biére de garde. Belgium is one of the few places that you will find spontaneously fermented sour ales such as lambic, gueuze, and Flanders red and brown, still brewed using traditional methods hundreds of years old.

When brewing Belgian-style beers pay attention to that notion of drinkability. Keep them dry, not sweet. Belgian beers should be highly attenuated. The use of simple sugars to supplement those from barley can help with this. Use a light hand with spices. You can always add more during conditioning if your kettle additions were not enough. Because yeast character is so important, attend to your fermentation. While some brewers have been known to push fermentation temperatures very high, keep in mind that every system is different. Yeast is impacted by many conditions including fermenter geometry. High temperatures may not be the right choice for your system.

Allagash Black
Allagash Brewing Company, Portland, Maine

From its founding in 1995 as a one-man operation, Allagash Brewing Company has grown into one of the most respected makers of Belgian-style ales in the United States. The brewery's lineup spans the range from a light and lively witbier to barrel-aged strong ales and spontaneously fermented sours. All bottled beers at Allagash are bottle conditioned. Allagash was one of the first in the country to use the traditional cork-and-cage closure.

Allagash Black is a complex Belgian-style stout that balances subdued, roasted-malt bitterness and dark chocolate flavors with the fruity and spicy character of Belgian yeast. Its silky-smooth texture is offset by a crisp, dry finish.

SPECIFICATIONS	OG: 1.072	FG: 1.015	ABV: 7.5%	IBU: 45	SRM: 38–40

Crush and steep in 2 gal. (7.5 L) of water at 160°F (71°C) for 30 minutes:

- 12 oz. (340 g) flaked oats
- 4 oz. (113 g) wheat malt
- 12 oz. (340 g) chocolate malt
- 3.2 oz. (91 g) black malt

Strain the grain into your brewpot and sparge with .5 gal. (2 L) 160°F (71°C) water. Add water as needed to bring the total volume to 2 gal. (7.5 L). Bring the water to a boil, remove from the heat, and add:

- 6.6 lb. (2.72 kg) pilsner liquid malt extract
- 4 oz. (.11 kg) light dry malt extract

Stir well until the extract is completely dissolved. Add water to bring the total volume to 3 gal. (11.3 L). Bring the wort to a rolling boil and add:

- 1.25 oz. (35.5 g) Perle hop pellets (9% AA)

Boil for 45 minutes and then add:

- 2 lb. (.9 kg) dark candy sugar rocks

Boil for another 30 minutes and then add:

- .5 oz. (14 g) Fuggles hop pellets (4.8% AA)

Remove from the heat and chill the wort as quickly as possible to below 80°F (27°C), using an ice bath or wort chiller. Transfer the wort to the fermenter and add cold water to bring the total volume to 5 gal. (19 L). Aerate the wort. Add the yeast:

- Wyeast 3787 Trappist High Gravity, Wyeast 3864 Canadian/ Belgian Ale, or WLP 500 Trappist Ale

Ferment at 65–70°F (18–21°C) until final gravity is achieved. Siphon to a secondary fermenter. Allow the beer to condition for 2 weeks. Bottle when fermentation is complete with:

- 6 oz. (170 g) corn sugar

ALL-GRAIN INSTRUCTIONS

Replace the malt extract with 9.75 lb. (4.42 kg) pilsner malt. Crush the grains and mash at 154°F (68°C) for 60 minutes. Sparge with 170°F (77°C) water until you reach a total volume of 6.25 gal. (23.7 L) in the brewpot. Reduce the 75-minute Perle hop addition to 1.05 oz. (29.76 g).

GOLD IN 2011 FOR CONFLUENCE AMERICAN- style ale. Gold in 2010 for Allagash Blonde, Belgian- and French-style ale, with silver and bronze medals for Sour and Witbier styles. Silver in 2009 (Belgian again). Gold and silver in 2006. Gold again, 2005, Belgian-style wheat.

If there's one thing Allagash knows, it's award-winning beer, particularly Belgian-style ales. The Allagash Brewing Company of Portland, Maine, began as a dream to fill a void in the craft brewing movement. Founder Rob Tod had experience working in breweries, and he recognized that although British and German styles had found their footing in America, the lighter Belgian styles and flavors hadn't quite landed on most beer drinkers' palates this side of the pond. He decided to start a modest fifteen-barrel brew house, and after selling his first batch in 1995—Allagash White, Tod's version of a Belgian traditional white beer, resplendent with hints of wheat, Curacao orange peel, coriander, and more—Allagash has continued pushing the limits of what a Belgian-style beer can be.

Allagash White is still the flagship beer of the company—the first style most newcomers to the brewery try—and in 2012, *Men's Journal* named it one of the top twenty-four beers in America. White is available year-round, as are five other distinctive styles in red, golden, and dark Belgian styles. Allagash also counts more than three dozen specialty, Tribute Series, limited-edition, collaboration, and draft-only beers to its name, mostly found at the brewery and specialty beer stores in New England. Allagash beers are strong, often pushing 8 to 10 percent ABV, as many of the specialty and limited-edition beers spend more than eighteen months fermenting. The Allagash Brewery tour has also been named one of the best in America.

Even the way the beer is stored and fermented pays tribute to old-world techniques. In 2001, Allagash began exploring the idea of cork- and cage-finished beers and bottle conditioning, more natural and time-sensitive ways to enhance flavor and quality. More than twenty-five years after its inception, Allagash continues to produce award-winning beers and expand its name and reputation outside the upper Atlantic coast. *—Jordan Wiklund*

Allagash Curieux
Allagash Brewing Company, Portland, Maine

Curieux was the first beer in Allagash's now-extensive barrel-aging program. It's made by aging the company's Tripel Ale in Jim Beam barrels for eight weeks. The aged beer is then blended with a portion of fresh tripel. The result is a beer of extraordinary depth. The cotton-candy and black pepper flavors of the tripel merge seamlessly with darker notes of vanilla, bourbon, and oak. This one is truly world-class.

SPECIFICATIONS	OG: 1.072	FG: 1.008	ABV: 9%	IBU: 35	SRM: 4.5–5

Crush and steep in .5 gal. (2 L) of water at 160°F (71°C) for 30 minutes:

- 4 oz. (113 g) Weyermann acidulated malt

Strain the grain into your brewpot and sparge with .5 gal. (2 L) of water at 160°F (71°C). Add water as needed to bring the total volume to 1.5 gal. (5.7 L). Bring the water to a boil, remove from the heat, and add:

- 6 lb. (2.72 kg) pilsner liquid malt extract
- 1.65 lb. (.74 kg) light dry malt extract

Stir well until the extract is completely dissolved. Add water to bring the total volume to 3 gal. (11.3 L). Bring the wort to a rolling boil and add:

- 1 oz. (28 g) Northern Brewer hop pellets (8% AA)

Boil for 45 minutes and then add:

- 2 lb. (.9 kg) dark candy sugar rocks

Boil for another 30 minutes and then add:

- 1.4 lb. (.64 kg) sucrose (table sugar)

Boil for another 15 minutes and then add:

- .5 oz. (14 g) Tettnang hop pellets (4.5% AA)

Remove from the heat and chill the wort as quickly as possible to below 80°F (27°C), using an ice bath or wort chiller. Transfer the wort to the fermenter and add cold water to bring the total volume to 5 gal. (19 L). Aerate the wort. Add the yeast:

- Wyeast 3787 Trappist High Gravity or WLP 500 Trappist Ale

Ferment at 65–70°F (18–21°C) until final gravity is achieved. Siphon to a secondary fermenter. Allow the beer to condition for 10 days at 40°F (4°C) and then add:

- Oak spirals soaked in Jim Beam bourbon whiskey for 10 days

Allow the beer to condition for 6 weeks at 40°F (4°C). Bottle when fermentation is complete with:

- 6 oz. (170 g) corn sugar

ALL-GRAIN INSTRUCTIONS

Replace the malt extract with 12.5 lb. (5.67 kg) pilsner malt. Crush the grains and mash at 152°F (67°C) for 60 minutes. Sparge with 170°F (77°C) water until you reach a total volume of 6.25 gal. (23.7 L) in the brewpot. Reduce the 75-minute Northern Brewer hop addition to .88 oz. (25 g).

Matacabras
Dave's BrewFarm, Wilson, Wisconsin

David Anderson isn't big on "style." When asked to describe one of his beers a normal response is, "You tell me." His goal, he says, is to expose people to what beer can be and then let them fill in the blanks. Taking inspiration from the brewers of Belgium, he employs herbs, spices, and other exotic ingredients to craft style-bending brews that aren't easily pegged. Matacabras is a perfect example of this way of brewing. Is it a Belgian barley wine or an English dubbel? Maybe it's an Anglo-Belgian imperial dunkel. Whatever you want to call it, Matacabras offers an ever-changing mix of flavors that roll riotously from one thing to another, at times resolving in articulated layers and at others collapsing together into a chaotic clump. It's one delightfully delicious trip.

SPECIFICATIONS	OG: 1.072	FG: 1.008	ABV: 8.5%	IBU: 38	SRM: 19

Crush and steep in 3 gal. (11.3 L) of water at 160°F (71°C) for 30 minutes:

- 1.75 lb. (.8 kg) Briess Rye malt
- 1.2 lb. (.54 kg) Dingemans Special B malt
- .7 oz. (19.84 g) Centennial hop pellets (10.5% AA)

Strain the grain into your brewpot and sparge with .5 gal. (2 L) of water at 160°F (71°C). Bring the water to a boil, remove from the heat, and add:

- 6 lb. (2.72 kg) light liquid malt extract
- 1.5 lb. (.68 kg) light dry malt extract

Stir well until the extract is completely dissolved. Add water to bring the total volume to 3 gal. (11.3 L). Bring the wort to a rolling boil. Boil for 30 minutes and then add:

- 8 oz. (225 g) dark brown sugar
- .5 oz. (14 g) Perle hop pellets (9% AA)

Boil for another 20 minutes and then add:

- .5 oz. (14 g) Millennium hop pellets (15.5% AA)

Boil for another 10 minutes and remove from heat. Chill the wort as quickly as possible to below 80°F (27°C), using an ice bath or wort chiller. Transfer the wort to the fermenter and add cold water to bring the total volume to 5 gal. (19 L). Aerate the wort. Add the yeast:

- Wyeast 3787 Trappist High Gravity

Ferment at 79°F (26°C) until final gravity is achieved. Siphon to a secondary fermenter. Allow the beer to condition for 2 weeks. Bottle when fermentation is complete with:

- 6 oz. (170 g) corn sugar

ALL-GRAIN INSTRUCTIONS

Replace the malt extract with 12 lb. (5.4 kg) Rahr pale two-row malt. Crush the grains and mash at 152°F (66°C) for 60 minutes. Sparge with 170°F (77°C) water until you reach a total volume of 6 gal. (22.7 L) in the brewpot. Reduce the Centennial hop addition to .55 oz. (15.6 g) and add to the kettle as the wort is being run off.

Saison
Funkwerks, Fort Collins, Colorado

A trip to Fort Collins, Colorado, should be near the top of every beer fan's to-do list. The picturesque college town is home to several breweries and brewpubs, ranging from the huge (Anheuser-Bush and New Belgium) to the tiny (Pateros Creek). Any visit to Fort Collins should include a stop at Funkwerks. Brewer Gordon Schuck focuses entirely on Belgian and French farmhouse-style ales. A sampler flight offers a smorgasbord of yeasty funkiness. The flagship Saison is super-dry with sharp, peppery spice notes from both yeast and hops. Light fruits round out the profile.

Becki Kregoski (www.bitesnbrews.com)

SPECIFICATIONS	OG: 1.055	FG: 1.005	ABV: 6.8%	IBU: 23	SRM: 4.2

Crush and steep in 2.25 gal. (8.5 L) of water at 160°F (71°C) for 30 minutes:

- 1.13 lb. (.5 kg) Gambrinus Munich 10L malt
- 1.13 lb. (.5 kg) Gambrinus Wheat malt

Strain the grain into your brewpot and sparge with .5 gal. (2 L) of water at 160°F (71°C). Bring the wort to a boil, remove from the heat, and add:

- 6 lb. (2.7 kg) pilsner liquid malt extract

Stir well until the extract is completely dissolved. Add water as needed to bring the total volume to 3 gal. (11.3 L). Bring the wort to a rolling boil then add:

- .8 oz. (22.68 g) Opal hop pellets (5.8% AA)

Boil for 45 minutes and then add:

- .6 oz. (17 g) Opal hop pellets (5.8% AA)

Boil for 15 minutes, remove from the heat, and then add:

- 1 oz. (28 g) Opal hop pellets (5.8% AA)

Chill the wort as quickly as possible to below 80°F (27°C), using an ice bath or wort chiller. Transfer the wort to the fermenter and add cold water to bring the total volume to 5 gal. (19 L). Aerate the wort. Add the yeast:

- Wyeast 3711 French Saison

Ferment at 70–72°F (21–22°C) until final gravity is achieved. Siphon to a secondary fermenter and add:

- .5 oz. (14 g) Opal hop pellets (5.8% AA)

Allow the beer to condition for 7 days. Bottle when fermentation is complete with:

- 6 oz. (170 g) corn sugar

ALL-GRAIN INSTRUCTIONS

Replace the malt extract with 9 lb. (4 kg) of Gambrinus pilsner malt. Crush the grains and mash in at 90°F (32°C). Raise the temperature to 145°F (63°F) and rest for 10 minutes. Raise the temperature to 158°F (70°C) and rest for 20 minutes. Mash out at 170°F (77°C). Sparge with 170°F (77°C) water until you reach a total volume of 6 gal. (22.7 L) in the brewpot. Reduce the 60-minute Opal hop addition to .7 oz. (19.85 g). Reduce the 15-minute Opal hop addition to .5 oz. (14 g).

FUNKWERKS
FORT COLLINS, COLORADO

FUNKWERKS is a relatively new microbrewery to the Colorado brewing scene. While that may deter some beer drinkers away to more lauded Colorado breweries like Odell and New Belgium, wise ale hunters will keep the Fort Collins brewery on their radar, because Funkwerks is doing just fine. More than fine, in fact. Within just a few years of selling its first batch, Funkwerks has carved out a niche for itself among Belgian-style aficionados, particularly those who love a spicy saison. Indeed, Funkwerks' Saison won silver in 2011 and gold in 2012 at the Great American Beer Festival in the French- and Belgian-style Saison category.

Not every brewery can claim top finishes within its first few years, but Funkwerks can, led by its flagship Funkwerks Saison.

But let's slow down a bit. What's a saison? Many people know what they like to drink without actually knowing what it is. Saison is a style of beer that originated in southern Belgium in the 1800s. Meaning "season" in French, saisons were typically brewed during the cold winter months and given to farmers during the hot summer season, when drinking water was questionable at best. The hops and spices in a good saison are bacteria-resistant and over time provide a wide variety of differentiation in color, texture, and flavor—just one of many reasons why saison-style beers are experiencing a comeback in America. No doubt part of that charge can be attributed to Funkwerks.

Funkwerks began with a one-barrel brewing system, but as recently as 2012, the brewery has added additional fermenters to its operation, doubling brewing capacity. The brewery sports an additional taproom, where other year-round beers and a few specialty beers can be sampled.

The Saison is described as "a tawny, orange-hued beer," with aromas of tangerine, passion fruit, and black pepper (pepper is a common flavor in many saisons). On the palate, flavors of orange, ginger, and lemon verbena explode, and the ale finishes with a "dry, lingering bitterness" that encourages another sip.

Other Funkwerks-brand beers include Deceit, which also won gold in the 2012 GABF for Belgian-style Strong Specialty Ale; Tropic King Imperial Saison, with hints of mango, peach, and passion fruit; Dark Prophet, a dark, barrel-aged Belgian composed of vanilla, cocoa, caramel, and more, perfect for those cold Colorado nights; and Solenna, a sweet and spicy, candy-apple Belgian-style beer. —*Jordan Wiklund*

Salvation
Avery Brewing Company, Boulder, Colorado

Avery's Belgian golden ale, Salvation, was introduced in 2002 as part of Avery's Holy Trinity of strong ales that also includes Hog Heaven Barleywine and The Reverend Belgian Style Quadrupel Ale. Salvation is a classic of the style. Sweet highlights of apricot and peach stone-fruit flavors intertwine with contrasting notes of herbs, cinnamon, and white pepper. The mouth-filling, cotton-candy character from the Belgian yeast strain gives a backdrop to both. It's a strong beer, but true to the Belgian way it remains light and drinkable.

SPECIFICATIONS	OG: 1.080	FG: 1.013	ABV: 8.9%	IBU: 33	SRM: 6.4

Crush and steep in 1 gal. (3.8 L) of water at 160°F (71°C) for 30 minutes:

- 10 oz. (284 g) Dingemans Cara-8 malt
- 10 oz. (284 g) Dingemans Cara-20 malt

Strain the grain into your brewpot and sparge with .5 gal. (2 L) of water at 160°F (71°C). Add water as needed to bring the total volume to 1.5 gal. (5.7 L). Bring the water to a boil, remove from the heat, and add:

- 6 lb. (2.7 kg) pilsner liquid malt extract
- 2.5 lb. (1.13 kg) light dry malt extract
- 14.5 oz. (411 g) light Belgian candy sugar

Stir well until the extract is completely dissolved. Add water to bring the total volume to 3 gal. (11.3 L). Bring the wort to a rolling boil then add:

- 1.4 oz. (39.7 g) Sterling hop pellets (5.5% AA)

Boil for 30 minutes and then add:

- .6 oz. (17 g) Sterling hop pellets (5.5% AA)

Boil for another 30 minutes, remove from the heat, and add:

- .8 oz. (23 g) Sterling hop pellets (5.5% AA)
- 2 oz. (57 g) Fuggles hop pellets (4.8% AA)

Chill the wort as quickly as possible to below 80°F (27°C), using an ice bath or wort chiller. Transfer the wort to the fermenter and add cold water to bring the total volume to 5 gal. (19 L). Aerate the wort. Add the yeast:

- Wyeast 3787 Trappist High Gravity or WLP530 Abbey Ale

Ferment at 68°F (20°C) for the first half of fermentation and then let the temperature rise as high as possible until final gravity is achieved. Siphon to a secondary fermenter. Allow the beer to condition for 7 days. Bottle when fermentation is complete with:

- 6 oz. (170 g) corn sugar

ALL-GRAIN INSTRUCTIONS

Replace the malt extract with 14.5 lb. (6.57 kg) pale two-row malt. Crush the grains and mash at 149°F (65°C) for 60 minutes. Sparge with 170°F (77°C) until you reach a total volume of 6 gal. (22.7 L) in the brewpot. Reduce the 60-minute Sterling hop addition to 1.2 oz. (34 g). Reduce the 30-minute Sterling hop addition to .4 oz. (11 g).

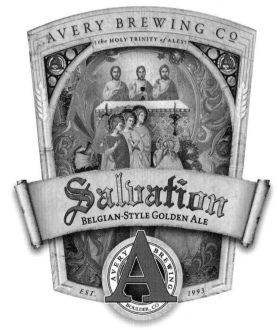

Scarlet 7
Red Eye Brewing Company, Wausau, Wisconsin

Among the breweries and brewpubs of Wausau, Wisconsin, Red Eye is unique. From the corrugated steel exterior to the sleek, modern design of the dining room, it suggests a place where art, food, and beer merge. Owner/brewer Kevin Eichelberger views his ingredients as colors on an artist's pallet. He has painted a palate-pleasing picture with Scarlet 7 Belgian Dubbel. A subtle Belgian yeast character underlies a body of caramel, burnt sugar, raisins, and figs. Bright cherry and clove notes bring contrasting colors.

BEER	STYLE	OG	IBU	ABV
BLOOM	BELGIAN WHEAT	11.9	10	5.1%
THRUST	AMERICAN IPA	15.5	59	6.5%
SCARLET 7	BELGIAN DUBBEL	17.0	15	7.0%
VERUCA STOUT	MILK STOUT	15.2	23	5.3%
CARA-AMBER WHEAT	AMERICAN DARK WHEAT	13.35	17	5.6%
NUT BROWN	SOUTHERN ENGLISH BROWN	13.6	13.8	5.3%

Scott D. Stephens (www.bayerntrips.com)

SPECIFICATIONS	OG: 1.070	FG: 1.013	ABV: 7.1%	IBU: 30	SRM: 21

Crush and steep in 4 gal. (4.5 L) of water at 160°F (71°C) for 30 minutes:

- 30 oz. (853 g) aromatic malt
- 15 oz. (425 g) Special B malt
- 15 oz. (425 g) Weyermann Munich malt
- 10 oz. (286 g) Simpsons Crystal 50L malt
- 2 oz. (57 g) Simpsons Crystal 155L malt

Strain the grain into your brewpot and sparge with .5 gal. (2 L) of water at 160°F (71°C). Bring the wort to a boil, remove from the heat, and add:

- 6 lb. (2.7 kg) light liquid malt extract

Stir well until the extract is completely dissolved. Add water as needed to bring the total volume to 3 gal. (11.3 L). Bring the wort to a rolling boil then add:

- .7 oz. (19.84 g) Willamette hop pellets (5.5% AA)

Boil for 30 minutes and then add:

- .7 oz. (19.84 g) Willamette hop pellets (5.5% AA)

Boil for 50 minutes and then add:

- 12 oz. (340 g) dextrose

Boil for 10 minutes and remove from the heat. Chill the wort as quickly as possible to below 80°F (27°C), using an ice bath or wort chiller. Transfer the wort to the fermenter and add cold water to bring the total volume to 5 gal. (19 L). Aerate the wort. Stabilize the temperature at 65°F (18°C). Add the yeast:

- WLP550 Belgian Ale

Allow the temperature to rise to 70°F (21°C) and maintain that temperature until final gravity is achieved. Siphon to a secondary fermenter. Allow the beer to condition for 7 days. Bottle when fermentation is complete with:

- 6 oz. (170 g) corn sugar

ALL-GRAIN INSTRUCTIONS

Replace the malt extract with 9 lb. (4 kg) of Rahr two-row pale malt. Crush the grains and mash at 152°F (67°C) for 60 minutes. Sparge with 170°F (77°C) water until you reach a total volume of 6.5 gal. (24.6 L) in the brewpot. Reduce the 90-minute Willamette hop addition to .6 oz. (17 g). Reduce the 30-minute Sterling hop addition to .6 oz. (17 g).

RED EYE BREWING COMPANY
WAUSAU, WISCONSIN

Scott D. Stephens (www.bayerntrips.com)

THE BREWERS OF RED EYE BREWING COMPANY see beer "as a painter would his palette, through which they manipulate grain, hops, yeast, and brewing techniques." At least, that's what the website says. You'll have to get to Wausau, Wisconsin, to find out for certain.

Red Eye is a small brewpub that boasts large flavor and ambitions. Currently, the brewpub offers four ales, but also something a little more for local Wisconsinites: a "commitment to the community and the environment, paired with sound economic practices."

Besides offering a couple of different ales (which we'll get to in a moment), Red Eye has made sustainability a part of its mission statement. Spent grain from the brewing processes is turned over to local farmers to support their cattle feeds, and the brewpub employs a variety of energy-conserving techniques in how it uses natural gas, electricity, and water. Red Eye uses energy-efficient appliances whenever feasible and promotes recycling efforts among its products and employees.

Naturally, many of Red Eye's patrons see eye-to-eye with the progressive brewing company and often find themselves at the brewpub enjoying one of four distinctive ales. Bloom is the name of Red Eye's flagship beer, a refreshing, orange-colored Belgian wheat. Next is Thrust! (with a deliberate exclamation point in the title), an American-style IPA. Scarlet 7 is inspired by Belgian dubbels of old, while peach wheat is exactly what it sounds like—a delicious, peachy wheat.

An organic food menu and restaurant abuts the brewpub, so a full sustainable dining experience is on hand for any wise enough to go there. Actively pursuing healthier menu options, Red Eye doesn't count a single fryer on its premises. The pizza dough, for example, is made fresh every day, using only basic ingredients: flour, salt, yeast, and the most natural ingredient of them all, water.

Though Red Eye is not widely distributed, the brewpub has found a fierce fandom through its high-quality practices, progressive and responsible outlook, and, of course, its delicious Belgian-style beers. —*Jordan Wiklund*

Saison Rue
The Bruery, Placentia, California

Patrick Rue (the "rue" in Bruery) started homebrewing as a diversion while attending law school. Over time his hobby grew. As his passion for beer-making waxed, his love of the law waned. In 2008 he left lawyering behind and opened the brewery. His mix of traditional and experimental Belgian-style beers caught on. The Bruery quickly gained a national reputation that far exceeded its diminutive size. The flagship Saison Rue well exemplifies what the Bruery does. The traditional Belgian/French farmhouse ale base is given an extra spicy kick from rye malt. Wild and funky Brettanomyces yeast added at bottling brings significant changes to the beer as it matures.

SPECIFICATIONS	OG: 1.072	FG: 1.008	ABV: 8.5%	IBU: 30	SRM: 10

Crush and steep in .5 gal. (2 L) of water at 160°F (71°C) for 30 minutes:

- 6 oz. (170 g) Bairds Brown malt
- .65 oz. (18.42 g) Magnum hop pellets (14% AA)

Strain the grain into your brewpot and sparge with .5 gal. (2 L) of water at 160°F (71°C). Bring the wort to a boil, remove from the heat, and add:

- 9.15 lb. (4.15 kg) rye liquid malt extract

Stir well until the extract is completely dissolved. Add water as needed to bring the total volume to 3 gal. (11.3 L). Bring the wort to a rolling boil. Boil for 40 minutes and then add:

- .15 oz. (4.25 g) spearmint

Boil for 15 minutes and then add:

- 9 oz. (255 g) corn sugar

Boil for 5 minutes and then add:

- .5 oz. (14 g) Sterling hop pellets (5.5% AA)

Remove from the heat. Chill the wort as quickly as possible to below 80°F (27°C), using an ice bath or wort chiller. Transfer the wort to the fermenter and add cold water to bring the total volume to 5 gal. (19 L). Stabilize the temperature at 65°F (18°C). Aerate the wort. Add the yeast:

- WLP570 Belgian Golden Ale

Let the temperature slowly rise to 85°F (29°C) over the course of fermentation. When final gravity is achieved, siphon to a secondary fermenter and allow the beer to condition for 5 to 7 days. Bottle when fermentation is complete with:

- WLP650 Brettanomyces bruxellensis
- 6 oz. (170 g) corn sugar

ALL-GRAIN INSTRUCTIONS

Replace malt extract with 9.25 lb. (4.2 kg) Great Western two-row pale malt and 4.4 lb. (2 kg) Weyermann rye malt. Crush the grains and mash at 150°F (66°C) for 60 minutes. Sparge with 170°F (77°C) water until you reach a total volume of 6 gal. (22.7 L) in the brewpot. Reduce the Magnum hop addition to .55 oz. (15.6 g).

5

OTHER ALES

Wow! Where to begin? Do we dive right in with a strong ale such as barleywine or old ale? Or do we start off light with a lager-like cream ale or blonde? Maybe we look to the Germans for a delicate Kölsch or an amber altbier. But then the brown ales, both the English and American varieties, catch our attention, while the Irish red and the Scottish ales speak up with brash bluster and demand to be tasted. And what about the specialty beers? Those unique creations of the brewer's imagination that defy easy categorization, those are tempting too. Where to begin?

The recipes that follow cover a range of styles from the American, English, and German traditions. Some stay fairly close to the guidelines, while others might be considered style benders.

English Styles

Odell's 90 Shilling is a classic Scottish ale. Hops don't grow in Scotland, so Scottish brewers had to import them from England. When the English started taxing hops, the Scots started making maltier beers. 90 Shilling features rich caramel malt with just enough hops to keep it balanced.

El Lector from Cigar City is brewed in the style of an English mild. In England the term "mild" used to refer simply to a beer that was served fresh. Aged beer was called "stale." Nowadays, mild is a subset of English brown ales. It's a malt-forward beer with notes of nuts and pumpernickel bread. Subtle, earthy hops round it out.

Oakshire Brewing's Ill-Tempered Gnome recalls the English winter warmers. This malty/hoppy ale is perfect for curling up by the fire on a cold winter's night.

German Styles

Blue Mountain Kölsch 151 is brewed in the kölsch style, a holdout from the days before lager brewing took over Germany. It is considered a hybrid style, because it's made with a top-fermenting yeast at lower temperatures than most ales. It also receives an extended period of cold lagering post-fermentation. According to the *Kölsch Konvention*, a true kölsch must be brewed within the city limits of Köln (Cologne), Germany. If you are sipping kölsch near the Cologne cathedral, be sure to tell the waiter when you are finished. An empty glass means you are ready for another.

Rogue Dead Guy Ale might be called a stylistic mashup. It's brewed in the style of a bock, but with an ale yeast. The result is a deliciously malty beer with a round, ale mouthfeel and light, fruity notes.

American Styles

The American beer industry has always been a style innovator. In this section you'll find three examples of iconic American beer styles: cream ale, American amber, and American brown.

Cream ale was American ale brewers' answer to the growing popularity of lagers. Like kölsch, it could be considered a hybrid brew in that it uses ale yeast at colder than usual temperatures. Like most American-made lager beers it typically includes some percentage of corn in the grist. Cream ale is great for those times when you just want something light. Xenu, Cigar City's take on the style, tweaks the classic with a touch of honey.

Amber ale is another truly American invention. Caramel malt leads the way in these delicious session beers with moderate but noticeable bitterness following along close behind. There are three different versions of the style represented here. Hellion from TRVE Brewing and Stone Brewing's Levitation Ale are both balanced, low-alcohol, session brews. Though located in Pennsylvania, Tröegs Brewing takes a West Coast approach to amber ale with Nugget Nectar, amping up both the IBU and the ABV.

American brown ale was invented by American homebrewers in search of a fuller-flavored version of the English classic. Appropriately, Rogue's Hazelnut Brown Nectar was originally based on a homebrewer's recipe. This nutty take on the style has become one of the Oregon brewery's bestselling beers.

90 Shilling Ale
Odell Brewing Company, Fort Collins, Colorado

Truly graybeards in the world of craft beer, Odell started in 1989 with two recipes cofounder Doug Odell had perfected in his kitchen, including Odell's flagship 90 Shilling. Odell Brewing grew over the years from a keg-only operation, eventually adding a bottling line and crafting 45,000 barrels a year. Conceived as a lighter version of a traditional Scottish ale, 90 Shilling is a smooth, medium-bodied amber. Its name, Odell explains, comes from the Scottish method of taxing beer—only the highest quality beers were taxed 90 shillings. —*Billy Broas*

SPECIFICATIONS	OG: 1.052	FG: 1.012	ABV: 5.3%	IBU: 27	SRM: 10

Crush and steep in 3 gal. (11.3 L) of 155°F (71°C) water for 45 minutes:

- 1 lb. (.45 kg) Munich 10L malt
- 8 oz. (225 g) Crystal 80L malt
- 8 oz. (225 g) Crystal 20L malt
- 8 oz. (225 g) wheat malt
- 8 oz. (225 g) Carapils malt

Bring the wort to a boil, remove from the heat, and add:

- 4 lb. (1.81 kg) light dry malt extract

Stir well until the extract is completely dissolved. Add water as needed to bring the total volume to 3 gal. (11.3 L). Bring the wort to a rolling boil then add:

- .6 oz. (17 g) Cascade hop pellets (6% AA)

Boil for 15 minutes and then add:

- .5 oz. (14 g) Cascade hop pellets (6% AA)

Boil for 15 minutes, remove from the heat, and then add:

- 1 oz. (28 g) Cascade hop pellets (6% AA)

Remove from the heat. Chill the wort as quickly as possible to 67°F (19°C), using an ice bath or wort chiller. Transfer the wort to the fermenter and add cold water to bring the total volume to 5 gal. (19 L). Aerate the wort. Add yeast:

- White Labs WLP007 Dry English Ale

Ferment at 67°F (19°C) until final gravity is achieved. Allow the beer to condition for seven days. Bottle when fermentation is complete with:

- 6 oz. (170 g) corn sugar

ALL-GRAIN INSTRUCTIONS

Replace the malt extract with 8 lb. (3.6 kg) of American two-row malt. Crush the grains and mash at 152°F (67°C). Sparge with 170°F (77°C) water to reach a total volume of 6 gal. (22.7 L) in the brewpot. Reduce the 60-minute Cascade hop addition to .5 oz. (14.17 g). Reduce the 30-minute Cascade hop addition to .4 oz. (11.34 g). Reduce the 15-minute Cascade hop addition to .9 oz. (25.51 g).

ODELL BREWING COMPANY

FORT COLLINS, COLORADO

YOU'VE PROBABLY HEARD OF Odell Brewing Company.

Odell has been around for a long time—since 1989, the dark ages before anyone was really talking about craft beer. Doug Odell had been homebrewing for more than ten years, refining recipe after recipe and slowly perfecting his own brewing process. He started the Odell Brewing Company with his wife, Wynne, and his sister, Corkie, when Colorado counted only one microbrewery within its mountainous borders.

Odell swung for the fences from the beginning and has been hitting home runs with its beers ever since. The flagship beer, 90 Shilling Ale, was one of Doug Odell's original and perfected beers since he first started homebrewing in the 1970s. Making sales calls out of his old Datsun, Odell peddled his beers around the state, not-so-quietly ringing in the start of the craft-beer era.

Since 2009, Odell has produced nearly 45,000 barrels annually and shows no signs of slowing down. In 2010, the Fort Collins brewery added a wood-aging cellar to its facilities, a 750-ml bottling line, and even a 76-kilowatt photovoltaic system, providing valuable and renewable energy to the brewery. The system counts for 25 percent of the brewery's energy needs. And like other breweries around the nation, Odell cites sustainability as one of its key goals. Three of its four biodiesel delivery trucks yield more energy than they consume, all its cardboard packaging is recyclable, and the brewery also recycles about 98 percent of its solid waste.

Odell sells six beers year-round, three seasonals, and more than a dozen others, all available at the brewery or in special limited editions in stores and on tap. The flagship 90 Shilling Ale and Easy Street Wheat remain huge hits wherever they're sold; 90 Shilling Ale is a lighter version of a traditional Scottish ale, smooth, medium-bodied, and amber in color. As for the name, 90 shillings was the Scottish tax for only the highest quality beers. Easy Street Wheat is a golden, unfiltered American-style wheat beer that has garnered no less than three Great American Brew Festival medals, winning gold in 1993 and 2005 and taking home an additional silver in 2007. At 4.6 percent ABV, it's recommended to kick back, take 'er easy, and enjoy its smooth, citrusy flavor in the company of friends.

Besides Colorado (all over it, in fact), Odell beer can be found in many stores, pubs, and restaurants in New Mexico, Arizona, Wyoming, Idaho, Kansas, Missouri, Nebraska, Minnesota, and South Dakota. Barring something catastrophic to the state of American brewing, Odell will be a name to remember for as long as good people still enjoy good beer. *—Jordan Wiklund*

Dead Guy Ale
Rogue Ales, Newport, Oregon

Rogue Ales was established in Ashland, Oregon, near the Rogue River, in 1988 as a 10 bbl. brewery and pub. In 1989, Rogue moved to the coastal town of Newport, Oregon, and John Maier came on board as brewmaster. Maier was the American Homebrewers Association Homebrewer of the Year in 1986 and had been working for the Alaskan Brewery before moving to Rogue. His homebrew roots are evident in some of the off-the-wall, over-the-top beers that Rogue brews. Dead Guy is not one of those. Created for a Portland restaurant for its Day of the Dead celebration, Dead Guy is Rogue's ale version of a German Maibock. It's got a great malt profile, but in true Rogue fashion it has a healthy dose of hops to back up the malt. It's a smooth, easy-drinking beer that has become a flagship brew for Rogue.

—*Denny Conn*

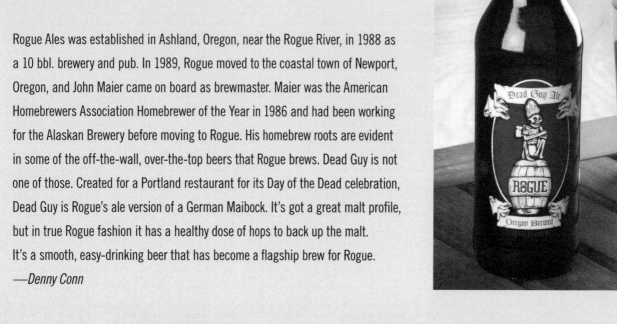

SPECIFICATIONS	OG: 1.065	FG: 1.015	ABV: 6.95%	IBU: 39.6	SRM: 13.5

Crush and steep in 2.25 gal. (8.5 L) of water at 155°F (68°C) for 60 minutes:

- 3.25 lb. (1.47 kg) Great Western Munich 10L malt
- 1.5 lb. (.68 kg) Great Western Crystal 15L malt

Strain the grain into your brewpot and sparge with 1 gal. (3.8 L) of water at 160°F (71°C). Bring the wort to a boil, remove from the heat, and add:

- 5 lb. (2.25 kg) light dry malt extract

Stir well until the extract is dissolved. Add water as needed to bring the volume to 3 gal. (11.3 L). Bring the wort to a rolling boil. Boil for 10 minutes, and then add:

- 1.15 oz. (32.6 g) Perle hop pellets (9% AA)

Boil for 60 minutes and then add:

- .5 oz. (14 oz.) Sterling hop pellets (5.5% AA)

Remove from the heat and let the hops steep for 10 minutes. Chill as quickly as possible to below 80°F (27°C). Transfer the wort to the fermenter and add cold water to bring the total volume to 5 gal. (19 L). The temperature should be below 70°F (21°C) at this point. Aerate wort and pitch an appropriately sized starter of:

- Wyeast 1764 Pacman

Ferment at 60–65°F (16–18°C) until final gravity is reached. You can either leave the beer in primary fermentation for 3 weeks or transfer to a secondary fermenter for a week after final gravity is reached in the primary. Bottle when fermentation is complete with:

- 4 oz. (113 g) corn sugar

ALL-GRAIN INSTRUCTIONS

Replace the extract with 10.25 lb. (4.65 kg) of Great Western two-row pale malt. Crush the grain and mash all grain at 152°F (67°C), using 5.75 gal. (21.8 L) of water. Sparge with enough water at 180°F (82°C) to reach your intended boil volume. Reduce the 60-minute Perle hop addition to 1 oz. (28.35 g).

ROGUE ALES
NEWPORT, OREGON

ROGUE ALES WAS FOUNDED IN 1988 in Ashland, Oregon, by a group of friends and their accountant, an avid homebrewer who, when he wasn't helping clients with taxes, was making beer to help them forget about them. The accountant, Jeff Schultz, convinced his client Bob Woodell to grab a few buddies—Jack Joyce and Rob Strasser, Oregon Ducks both—and Rogue Ales was born.

Never has mixing business with pleasure been more successful.

Since the sale of its first batch of beer, Rogue Ales has become one of the most recognized microbrew brands in America, operating three distinct brewpubs in Oregon, Washington, and California, and even opening micro distilleries in both Newport and Portland. Rogue has produced more than sixty ales and continues to push the boundaries of microbrew styles and flavors.

Brewmaster John "More Hops" Maier has been with the company since 1989. He graduated from the Siebel Institute of Technology in 1986, winning the American Homebrewer Association's Homebrewer of the Year Award a few months later. Since then, Maier has garnered more than 500 awards for his vision and excellence in brewing.

Rogue's Dead Guy Ale is one of the most recognizable microbrews on the market today. First conceived in the early 1990s to celebrate the Mayan Day of the Dead, the design for Dead Guy became almost as popular as the beer itself. Featuring a grinning skeleton sitting atop a barrel of beer with a frosty glass in his skeletal hand, the Dead Guy has been gracing liquor stores and pubs around the nation for years.

Dead Guy Ale is a German-style maibock, described as "deep honey in color, with a malty aroma and a rich hearty flavor." Dead Guy *alone* has won more than twenty-five World Beer and other festival awards for its malty goodness and clean finish.

Rogue believes that variety is the spice of life and is proud to produce its ales using a nonpasteurized process without preservatives, meaning no two batches are quite the same. Only all-natural ingredients are used.

In recent years, Rogue's darker side has seen some of the limelight. Recent Great American Beer Festival award winners include Smoke Ale (Smoke Beer category); Hazelnut Brown Nectar (Specialty Beer); Shakespeare Oatmeal Stout (American-style Stout); Imperial Chocolate Stout (Herb and Spice or Chocolate Beer); and Mocha Porter (Robust Porter).

Light or dark, old or new, Rogue has something for every place and palate and for every guy sitting atop a beer barrel, brew in hand. —*Jordan Wiklund*

El Lector
Cigar City Brewing, Tampa, Florida

Cigar City founder Joey Redner named his brewery in homage to the history and culture of its hometown, Tampa, Florida, once the world's largest producer of cigars. The city's Latin roots run deep and meld with the customs of the diverse people who live there to create a unique culture that's all its own. This diversity is reflected in Cigar City's beers. The brewery is best known for the exotically spiced Hunahpu's Imperial Stout or the Humidor Series beers that are aged in Spanish cedar, but its lineup includes many less adventurous but still finely crafted brews. El Lector English-style dark mild ale is one such beer. This draft-only beer is the brewery's smallest offering. Staying true to its English roots, it features pronounced caramel and toasted malt flavors with background hints of roast and nuts.

Chris O'Meara (AP Images)

SPECIFICATIONS	OG: 1.048	FG: 1.018	ABV: 4%	IBU: 18	SRM: 20

Crush and steep in 2 gal. (7.5 L) of water at 160°F (71°C) for 30 minutes:

- 1.15 lb. (522 g) Caramel 40L malt
- 5 oz. (142 g) chocolate malt
- 3 oz. (85 g) flaked barley
- 2 oz. (57 g) Caramel 20L malt
- 2 oz. (57 g) Dingemans Special B malt

Strain the grain into your brewpot and sparge with .5 gal. (2 L) of water at 160°F (71°C). Bring the water to a boil, remove from the heat, and add:

- 3.15 lb. (1.43 kg) Maris Otter liquid malt extract
- 1.75 lb. (.8 kg) light dry malt extract

Stir well until the extract is completely dissolved. Add water to bring the total volume to 3 gal. (11.3 L). Bring the wort to a rolling boil then add:

- .3 oz. (8.5 g) Magnum hop pellets (14% AA)

Boil for 60 minutes and then add:

- .5 oz. (14 g) Fuggles hop pellets (4.8% AA)

Remove from the heat and chill the wort as quickly as possible to below 80°F (27°C), using an ice bath or wort chiller. Transfer the wort to the fermenter and add cold water to bring the total volume to 5 gal. (19 L). Aerate the wort. Add the yeast:

- Wyeast 1275 Thames Valley Ale

Ferment at 66°F (19°C) until final gravity is achieved. Siphon to a secondary fermenter and allow the beer to condition for 7 to 10 days. Bottle when fermentation is complete with:

- 6 oz. (170 g) corn sugar

ALL-GRAIN INSTRUCTIONS

Replace the malt extract with 8 lb. (3.63 kg) of Crisp Maris Otter malt. Crush the grains and mash at 158° F (70° C) for 60 minutes. Sparge with 170°F (79°C) water to reach a total volume of 6 gal. (22.7 L) in the kettle. Reduce the 60-minute Magnum hop addition to .26 oz. (7.37 g).

Chris O'Meara (AP Images)

CIGAR CITY BREWING
TAMPA, FLORIDA

Brendan Farrington (AP Images)

WITH TWO GOALS IN MIND, Cigar City Brewing has its path set: first, to make the world's best beer (which many in Tampa already believe they've done), and second, to share with that world the diverse culture and rich heritage of Tampa. From its Latin roots to its history as the largest cigar producer on the planet, Tampa has much to offer, including this no-nonsense brewery.

Cigar City Brewing is a fifteen-barrel brew house that features nineteen fermenters using the highest quality ingredients to make beer within 6,600 square feet of warehouse space in the Carver City/Lincoln Gardens neighborhood of Tampa. Head brewer Wayne Wambles and the Cigar City team believe that "beer should reflect the environment in which it is made and as such should have a sense of purpose." With that in mind, don't be surprised when you read about nontraditional ingredients borne of a love for local Tampa culture, including (but not limited to) guava, hints of cigar box cedar, and the fruity aromas that waft to and fro from the best and brightest fruit gardens of Florida.

For this reason, it should come as no surprise that Cigar City Brewing has enjoyed wide acclaim in the few short years it has been open since 2009. Each year since then, Cigar City has medaled at the Great American Beer Festival, receiving two golds, one silver, and a bronze, in the categories of Extra Special Bitter, Wood- and Barrel-aged, and Field or Pumpkin beer.

If you're only passing through Florida and don't have time to swing by Cigar City's taproom, find the right concourse and set your path appropriately: Cigar City is opening a small expansion in the Tampa International Airport, giving TIA the distinction of being the first airport in the country to sell beer brewed on site.

So no matter how, when, or why you get to Florida, you don't have any more excuses to miss out on some of the best craft beer in the South (much less the nation). —*Jordan Wiklund*

Hazelnut Brown Nectar
Rogue Ales, Newport, Oregon

Rogue Ales brewmaster John Maier started out as a homebrewer, so it's
not surprising that he and Rogue have always been big supporters of
homebrewers. Several of Rogue's most popular recipes have homebrew roots,
and its Hazelnut Brown Nectar is one of the best examples. From a recipe
created by Chris Studach of the Cascade Brewers Society in Eugene, Oregon,
Hazelnut Brown Nectar has turned into one of Rogue's most popular beers,
winning many awards worldwide. The picture on the bottle is a caricature of
Chris, giving rise to the beer's nickname "Bald Guy Brown."—*Denny Conn*

SPECIFICATIONS	OG: 1.057	FG: 1.016	ABV: 5.6%	IBU: 25	SRM: 26.2

Crush and steep in 2.75 gal. (10.4 L) of water at 152°F (67°C) for 60 minutes:

- 2 lb. (.9 kg) Great Western Munich 10L malt
- 1.5 lb. (680 g) Great Western Crystal 75L malt 75L
- 9 oz. (255 g) Great Western Crystal 15L malt
- 9 oz. (255 g) Great Western Crystal 120L malt
- 11 oz. (312 g) Baird Brown malt
- 4 oz. (113 g) Franco-Belges Kiln Coffee malt

Strain the grain into your brewpot and sparge with 1 gal. (3.8 L) of water at 160°F (71°C). Bring the wort to a boil, remove from the heat, and add:

- 3.75 lb. (1.7 kg) light dry malt extract

Stir well until the extract is dissolved. Add water as needed to bring the volume to 3 gal. (11.3 L). Bring the wort to a rolling boil. Boil for 10 minutes, and then add:

- .7 oz. (19.84 g) Perle hop pellets (9% AA)

Boil for 60 minutes and then add:

- .5 oz. (14 g) Sterling hop pellets (5.5% AA)

Remove from the heat and let the hops steep for 10 minutes. Chill as quickly as possible to below 80°F (27°C). Transfer the wort to the fermenter and add cold water to bring the total volume to 5 gal. (19 L). The temperature should be below 70°F (21°C) at this point. Aerate wort and pitch an appropriately sized starter of:

- Wyeast 1764 Pacman

Ferment at 60–65°F (16–18°C) until final gravity is reached. You can either leave the beer in primary for 3 weeks or transfer to a secondary fermenter for a week after final gravity is reached in the primary. Bottle when fermentation is complete with:

- 4 oz. (113 g) corn sugar
- ½ tsp. Northwestern hazelnut extract

ALL-GRAIN INSTRUCTIONS

Replace the extract with 7.75 lb. (3.5 kg) Great Western two-row pale malt. Crush the grain and mash all grain at 152°F (67°C), using 5.75 gal. (21.8 L) of water. Sparge with enough water at 180°F (82°C) to reach your intended boil volume. Reduce the 60-minute Perle hop addition to .6 oz. (17.1 g).

SPECIAL INSTRUCTIONS

According to John Maier, brewmaster at Rogue Ales, Northwestern hazelnut extract is more potent than other brands. If you use another brand, you'll have to add it gradually at packaging and taste to ascertain the proper amount.

Hellion
TRVE Brewing, Denver, Colorado

Founded in 2011, TRVE (think of those legends chiseled over the entrances to ancient Greek buildings; in other words, think *true*) prides itself on disavowing set or expected guidelines when it comes to ingredients and styles. Witness Hellion, a unique American session ale loaded down with oats—more than three-quarters of a pound in the case of TRVE's 5-gallon batch. As TRVE bluntly proclaims in describing this summer lawnmower beer, it's a brew "you can drink the shit out of without worrying about your ability to remember which way's up. Notes of strawberry, blueberry, and a subtle lingering bitterness." Before you dive in, take note that this recipe must be made as either partial mash or all-grain. —*Billy Broas*

Sean Buchan (www.beertographer.com)

Sean Buchan (www.beertographer.com)

SPECIFICATIONS	OG: 1.041	FG: 1.010	ABV: 4.0%	IBU: 30	SRM: 11

Heat 2 gal. (7.5 L) of water to 152°F (67°C). Crush and add grains in a nylon-mesh bag. The temperature should be within a degree or two of 149°F (65°C). Maintain that temperature and steep for 60 minutes:

- 1 lb. (.45 kg) American two-row malt
- 1.5 lb. (.68 kg) Munich II malt
- 13 oz. (369 g) Simpsons Golden Naked Oats
- 6 oz. (170 g) Crystal 60L malt

While the mash rests, heat 1 gal. (3.8 L) of water to 168°F (76°C) in a separate pot. When the mash is finished, return the pot to the heat and slowly raise the temperature to 168°F (76°C). Strain the grain into your brewpot, and sparge with the water from the second pot. Bring the wort to a boil, remove from the heat, and add:

- 3.15 lb. (1.43 kg) pale liquid malt extract
- .75 lb. (.34 kg) light dry malt extract

Stir well until the extract is completely dissolved. Add water as needed to bring the total volume to 3 gal. (11.3 L). Bring the wort to a rolling boil then add:

- .45 oz. (12.75 g) Columbus pellet hops (15% AA)

Boil for 60 minutes, turn off the heat, and add:

- .3 oz. (9 g) Centennial pellet hops (10.5% AA)

Chill the wort as quickly as possible to 66°F (19°C), using an ice bath or wort chiller. Transfer the wort to the fermenter and add cold water to bring the total volume to 5 gal. (19 L). Aerate the wort. Add the yeast:

- White Labs WLP001 California Ale

Ferment at 66°F (19°C) until final gravity is achieved.

Allow the beer to condition for 1 week. Bottle with:

- 5 oz. (140 g) corn sugar

ALL-GRAIN INSTRUCTIONS

Replace the malt extract with 6 lb. (2.72 kg) American two-row malt for a total of 7 lb. (3.17 kg). Crush the grains and mash at 149°F (65°C) for 60 minutes. Sparge with 168°F (76°C) water to reach a total volume of 6 gal. (22.7 L) in the brewpot. Reduce the 60-minute Columbus hop addition to .4 oz. (11.34 g).

TRVE BREWING
DENVER, COLORADO

Sean Buchan (www.beertographer.com)

TRVE (PRONOUNCED "TRUE") BREWING was founded during the summer solstice of 2011. A raging, roaring peal of thunder ripped across the Colorado sky as the silhouette of a pale horseman could be seen through the rain, wind, and moonlight. He raised a bony hand, summoning the most fervent beer drinkers and homebrewers in all the mountainous land, chanting long-forgotten, infernal brewing incantations to the dark lord of barley and hops.

OK, it may not have happened *quite* like that, but TRVE Brewing was indeed founded on that warm summer night, inspired by and brewed for lovers of black metal and good, good beer. The mission, according to the company website, "has always been to create beers that are beyond the pale . . . channeling Loki and embracing chaos." Self-described "style blasphemers and category agnostics," TRVE Brewing has something for every saint and sinner.

Founder and homebrewer Nick Nunns is proud that the beers and people behind TRVE Brewing represent "being a part of a counter culture without immersing yourself to the point of taking it too seriously." From behind one of the longest single tables in Colorado—a 30-foot oaken beauty on the main floor of his taproom—he pours beer produced in a 250-square-foot brew house behind the bar, where his three-barrel system is housed. With a smaller system, Nunns believes he can exercise greater flexibility among the flavors and styles of his beers and eschew traditional guidelines if they brew up something worth saving.

All of TRVE Brewing's beers are named after famous black metal songs or albums. From the 4 percent summer seasonal Prehistoric Dog wheat all the way up the ABV scale to the 10 percent Nazareth double IPA, the beers are intended to challenge and invigorate the senses, defying what typical beer drinkers may think of as a standard IPA, saison, or stout. Hellion, an American table beer, is a local favorite; at 4.4 percent ABV, it's a beer "you can drink the shit out of," according to the website.

But don't stop there. With a constantly changing lineup of six to eight beers on tap and more available in special-edition or limited batches, there's always something new to try at TRVE Brewing's busy Baker neighborhood locale in Fort Collins. —*Jordan Wiklund*

Ill-Tempered Gnome
Oakshire Brewing, Eugene, Oregon

Oakshire Brewing's Ill-Tempered Gnome is a winter seasonal beer that almost makes you glad the rain has started in Oregon. Breaking the mold of a winter seasonal, Ill-Tempered Gnome uses no herbs, spices, or flavorings. The OG is healthy but not insane. It's a malty, hoppy glass of goodness to curl up with when the rain sets in and the days are cold and dark. —*Denny Conn*

Matt Wiater (www.portlandbeer.com)

Matt Wiater (www.portlandbeer.com)

SPECIFICATIONS	OG: 1.064	FG: 1.012	ABV: 6.8%	IBU: 65	SRM: 22

Crush and steep in 2.25 gal. (8.5 L) of water at 155°F (68°C) for 30 minutes:

- 11 oz. (312 g) Crystal 15L malt
- 4.5 oz. (128 g) Briess Special Roast malt
- 5 oz. (142 g) Special B malt
- 5 oz. (142 g) honey malt
- 5 oz. (142 g) Franco-Belges Kiln Coffee malt
- 3.5 oz. (99 g) chocolate malt

Strain the grain into your brewpot and sparge with .5 gal. (2 L) of water at 160°F (71°C). Bring the wort to a boil, remove from the heat, and add:

- 5.85 lb. (2.65 kg) light dry malt extract

Note: For best results, add gypsum to bring the sulfate level of your water to 120 ppm. If you don't know your base sulfate level, add 1 rounded tsp. (5 g) of gypsum if you have soft water. Don't add gypsum if you have hard water.

Stir well until the extract is dissolved. Add water as needed to bring the volume to 3 gal. (11.3 L). Bring the wort to a rolling boil. Boil for 10 minutes, and then add:

- 1.17 oz. (33 g) Nugget hop pellets (13% AA)

Boil for 40 minutes and then add:

- .35 oz. (10 g) Centennial hop pellets (10.5% AA)
- .35 oz. (10 g) Crystal hop pellets (4.5% AA)

Boil for 20 minutes and then add:

- .6 oz. (17 g) Cascade hop pellets (6% AA)

Remove from the heat and chill as quickly as possible to below 80°F (27°C). Transfer the wort to the fermenter and add cold water to bring the total volume to 5 gal. (19 L). The temperature should be below 70°F (21°C) at this point. Aerate wort and pitch an appropriately sized starter of:

- White Labs WLP001 California Ale or Wyeast 1056 American Ale

Ferment at 65–67°F (18–19°C) until final gravity is reached. Bottle with:

- 5 oz. (140 g) corn sugar

ALL-GRAIN INSTRUCTIONS

Replace extract with 12 lb. (5 kg) Great Western or Rahr two-row pale malt. Crush and mash all grain at 154°F (67°C) for 60 minutes. Sparge with 170°F (79°C) water to reach a total volume of 6.25 gal. (23.7 L) in the kettle. Reduce the 60-minute Nugget hop addition to 1 oz. (27 g). Reduce the 20-minute Centennial and Crystal hop additions to .3 oz. (8 g). Follow recommendations in the note above for the sulfate level.

Imperial Red Ale
Marble Brewery, Albuquerque, New Mexico

Marble Brewery has been producing rock-solid beer in Albuquerque, New Mexico, since 2008. It didn't take long for their hard work and dedication to pay dividends when their Imperial Red Ale took the silver medal at the 2012 Great American Beer Festival. A full-bodied beer that manages great complexity with a simple malt bill, it is balanced by an amazing combination of hops that can make you forget the fact that this big beer comes in at 9 percent ABV. —*Matthew Schaefer*

SPECIFICATIONS	OG: 1.084	FG: 1.012	ABV: 9%	IBU: 135	SRM: 25

Crush and steep in 3 gal. (11.3 L) of water at 160°F (71°C) for 30 minutes:

- 1.25 lb. (.57 kg) Crystal 75L malt
- 14 oz. (397 g) Crystal 120L malt
- 1.2 oz. (34.2 g) Centennial hop pellets (10.5% AA)
- 1.2 oz. (34.2 g) Chinook hop pellets (13% AA)
- 1.2 oz. (34.2 g) El Dorado hop pellets (13% AA)
- 1.2 oz. (34.2 g) Simcoe hop pellets (13% AA)

Remove the grain (leaving the hops behind) and sparge with .5 gallon (2 L) of water at 160°F (71°C). Bring the water to a boil, remove from the heat, and add:

- 12 lb. (5.4 kg) pale liquid malt extract

Stir well until the extract is completely dissolved. Add water to bring the total volume to 4 gal. (15.14 L), then bring the wort to a rolling boil for 30 minutes and add:

- 5 oz. (141.75 g) Centennial hop pellets (10.5% AA)

Remove from the heat and chill the wort as quickly as possible to below 80°F (27°C), using an ice bath or wort chiller. Transfer the wort to the fermenter and add cold water to bring the total volume to 5.5 gal. (20.8 L). Aerate the wort. Add the yeast:

- Wyeast 1056 American Ale, White Labs WLP001 California Ale, or Safale US-05

Ferment at 62°F (17°C) until final gravity is achieved. Siphon to a secondary fermenter and then add:

- 3.25 oz. (92 g) Sorachi Ace hop pellets (12% AA)
- .65 oz. (18.4 g) Chinook hop pellets (13% AA)
- .65 oz. (18.4 g) Simcoe hop pellets (13% AA)

Allow the beer to condition on the dry hops for 7 days. Bottle when fermentation is complete with:

- 5 oz. (140 g) corn sugar

ALL-GRAIN INSTRUCTIONS

Replace the malt extract with 14.7 lb. (6.52 kg) of two-row pale ale malt. Crush the grains and mash at 150° F (66° C) for 60 minutes. Sparge with 170°F (79°C) water to reach a total volume 6.5 gal. (24.6 L) in the brewpot for a 60-minute boil. Reduce the Centennial, Chinook, El Dorado, and Simcoe first wort hop additions to .69 oz. (19.56 g). Reduce the 30-minute Centennial hop addition to 2.7 oz. (76.5 g).

SPECIAL INSTRUCTIONS

This recipe calls for a larger boil and ending volume to account for the significant amount of liquid that is going to be lost to the hops, which will soak up wort during the boil and during dry hopping.

THE SOUTHWEST IS GENERALLY REGARDED as an arid, dry region, but you wouldn't know it from the work and brews of Marble Brewery of Albuquerque, New Mexico. Founded by Jeff Jinnett, Ted Rice, and John Gozigian, Marble Brewery has a mission to provide high-quality beers and an informal atmosphere appropriate for young and old, hipster and business person alike.

Luckily for Marble, that hasn't been a problem.

Marble draws its namesake from Marble Avenue, located in the northern warehouse district of Albuquerque. Since its opening, the Marble Brewery has become a community hub for city workers, students, artists, and more. Marble offers seven beers year-round at the brewery and its two off-site taprooms in Santa Fe and western Albuquerque. Several more seasonal and specialty varieties are available in limited batches at all three locations.

Founded in 2008, the Marble Brewery has enjoyed a well-deserved reputation as one of the best breweries of the Four Corners states.

The motto of the brewery is "Rock. Solid. Beer." Beer aficionados tend to agree; since 2008, Marble has scored three medals at the Great American Beer Festival for its Pilsner, Imperial Red, and Double White ales. Marble brews well, and Marble brews strong—none of its regular beers clock in at anything less than about 4.8 percent ABV. The IPA rates at a hearty 6.8 percent ABV, while the Double IPA makes a cool 8.0 percent ABV. In recent years, Lambert's Pale Ale garnered first place at the New Mexico State Fair beer competition.

Albuquerque is known for its beauty, culture, and rich cultural heritage. The Marble Brewery is rapidly making Albuquerque synonymous with "damn good beer." —*Jordan Wiklund*

Kölsch 151
Blue Mountain Brewery, Afton, Virginia

Virginia-based Blue Mountain is one of the growing numbers of craft brewers taking an active interest in issues of sustainability, including treating wastewater before discharging it. In addition, Blue Mountain takes its water from an onsite well fed by the surrounding watershed and maintains a hop farm featuring 500 rhizomes of Cascades and Centennials. The Blue Mountain staff notes that Virginia was once known as the "hop capital of the new world." That said, Blue Mountain's Kölsch 151 has a decidedly old-world flare. Though this a style of ale indigenous to Cologne, Germany, Blue Mountain treats its Kölsch like a lager, giving it an extensive cold-aging process to produce a clean, crisp beer. German Pilsen and Vienna malts and Hallertau-region hops lend a balanced flavor. —*Billy Broas*

SPECIFICATIONS	OG: 1.050	FG: 1.012	ABV: 5.0%	IBU: 17	SRM: 4

Crush and steep in 1 gal. (3.8 L) of 150°F (66°C) water for 45 minutes:

- 13 oz. (369 g) Vienna malt
- 3 oz. (85 g) Crystal 10L malt

Remove the grain into your brewpot. Bring the wort to a boil, remove from the heat, and add:

- 3.65 lb. (1.65 kg) Pilsen dry malt extract
- 1.25 lb. (.56 kg) wheat dry malt extract

Stir well until the extract is completely dissolved. Add water as needed to bring the total volume to 3 gal. (11.3 L). Bring the wort to a rolling boil then add:

- .25 oz. (7.08 g) Perle hop pellets (9% AA)

Boil for 30 minutes and then add:

- .2 oz. (5.7 g) Perle hop pellets (9% AA)

Boil for 15 minutes and then add:

- .2 oz. (5.7 g) Perle hop pellets (9% AA)

Boil for 10 minutes and then add:

- .2 oz. (5.7 g) Perle hop pellets (9% AA)

Boil for 5 more minutes and then chill the wort as quickly as possible to 66°F (19°C), using an ice bath or wort chiller. Transfer the wort to the fermenter and add cold water to bring the total volume to 5 gal. (19 L). Aerate the wort. Add the yeast.

- Wyeast 2565 Kölsch

Ferment at 66°F (19°C) until final gravity is achieved.

Allow the beer to condition for 7 days. Bottle when fermentation is complete with:

- 6 oz. (170 g) corn sugar

ALL-GRAIN INSTRUCTIONS

Replace the pilsner malt extract with 7.5 lb. (3.4 kg) of German pilsner malt. Replace the wheat malt extract with 1.5 lb. (.68 kg) of white wheat malt. Crush the grains and mash at 150°F (66°C) for 75 minutes. Sparge with 170°F (77°C) water to reach a total volume 6 gal. (22.7 L) in the brewpot. Reduce the 60-minute Perle hop addition to .2 oz. (5.7 g).

BLUE MOUNTAIN BREWERY
AFTON, VIRGINIA

Damien Dawson (AP Images)

WHAT ELSE IS THERE TO DO for a former head brewer for one of the most recognized beer brands in the country?

Start your own brewery, of course.

That's the story for Taylor Smack, former head brewer of both Goose Island brewpub in Chicago and South Street Brewery in Virginia. After more than a decade of experience between those two excellent brewpubs, Taylor decided it was time to open his own brewery in the shadow of the Blue Ridge Mountains in Afton, Virginia. Since 2007, Taylor has called the Blue Mountain Brewery home.

Once known as the "Hop Capital of the New World," all Blue Mountain hops are grown on brewpub site grounds, lending an unbelievable freshness that is second to none in all Blue Mountain beers. Once harvested in July or August, those hops often make their way to the onsite fifteen-by-thirty-barrel brewing system, where about 80,000 gallons (about 2,500 barrels) of beer are brewed each year. The water supplying the hops is local and all natural too. It comes from a 300-foot well and is fed by miles of pristine, untainted forest water that forms the rear slope of Blue Mountain's Appalachian site.

Blue Mountain beer can be found in much of the upper East Coast, from its home state of Virginia north to New York and Maryland, and even as far west as Michigan. Eight to ten styles of beer are typically available on tap and in bottles and cans, and a whopping twenty varieties of seasonal and limited-edition beers are available on the brewpub site year round.

One of the local favorites is a light, German-style ale called Kolsch 151. Treated like a lager, Kolsch 151 undergoes "extensive cold aging to produce a clean, crisp beer." At 5 percent ABV, Kolsch is a good choice any time of year (although it may be particularly refreshing during those long summer nights). Shortly after it debuted, Kolsch took home bronze in the 2010 Great American Beer Festival in the German-style Kolsch category. Other award-winning lighter ales include Summer Lovin', a gold-winning English-style summer ale at the GABF in 2011, and Sandy Bottom, another gold-winning ale, this time in 2010 for American-style Wheat.

If darker ales are your pleasure, you can't go wrong with Evil 8 Belgian-style Dubbel or the Dark Hollow Artisanal Ale, two beers as black as the fertile Virginia soil (and a whole hell of a lot tastier). No matter your choice, Blue Mountain is an East Coast staple of savvy beer drinkers. —*Jordan Wiklund*

Levitation
Stone Brewing Company, Escondido, California

There are few names bigger in craft beer than Stone Brewing, a brewery known for bold, assertive beers that pull no punches. Levitation proves that Stone Brewing can make a session beer with as much flavor and style as its bigger brethren. Coming in at just 4.5 percent ABV, Levitation is a beer that packs a lot of flavor and depth into a "small" package. —*Matthew Schaefer*

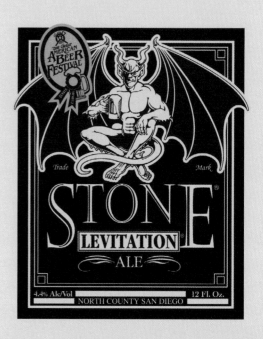

SPECIFICATIONS	OG: 1.048	FG: 1.013	ABV: 4.5%	IBU: 45	SRM: 18

Crush and steep in 1 gal. (3.78 L) of water at 160°F (71°C) for 30 minutes:

- 11.2 oz. (318 g) Crystal 75L malt
- 6.4 oz. (181 g) Crystal 150L malt
- 1 oz. (28 g) Black Patent malt

Strain the grain into your brewpot and sparge with .5 gallon (2 L) of water at 160°F (71°C). Bring the water to a boil, remove from the heat, and add:

- 6.5 lb. (2.95 kg) pale liquid malt extract

Stir well until the extract is completely dissolved. Add water to bring the total volume to 3 gal. (11.3 L). Bring the wort to a rolling boil then add:

- .5 oz. (14.17 g) Columbus hop pellets (15% AA)

Boil for 80 minutes and then add:

- 1.2 oz. (34 g) Amarillo hop pellets (9.5% AA)

Boil for 10 more minutes. Remove from the heat and then add:

- .9 oz. (25.5 g) Crystal hop pellets (4.5% AA)
- .9 oz. (25.5 g) Simcoe hop pellets (13% AA)

Chill the wort as quickly as possible to below 80°F (27°C), using an ice bath or wort chiller. Transfer the wort to the fermenter and add cold water to bring the total volume to 5 gal. (19 L). Aerate the wort. Add the yeast:

- White Labs WLP007 Dry English Ale or WLP002 English Ale

Ferment at 72°F (22°C) until final gravity is achieved. Siphon to a secondary fermenter and add:

- .77 oz. (22 g) Amarillo hop pellets (9.5% AA)

Allow the beer to condition for 7 days. Bottle when fermentation is complete with:

- 5 oz. (140 g) corn sugar

ALL-GRAIN INSTRUCTIONS

Replace the malt extract with 9.25 lb. (4.19 kg) of two-row pale ale malt. Crush the grains and mash at 157°F (69°C) for 60 minutes. Sparge with 170°F (79°C) water to reach a total volume of 6.5 gal. (24.6 L) in the brewpot for a 90-minute boil. Reduce the 90-minute Columbus hop addition to .43 oz. (12.2 g) and the 10-minute Amarillo addition to 1.1 oz. (31.18 g).

STONE BREWING COMPANY

ESCONDIDO, CALIFORNIA

ARE YOU LOOKING FOR the best brewery on Earth?

Look no further. According to websites RateBeer and BeerAdvocate, the Stone Brewing Company, of Escondido, California, is the best brewery on Earth. Literally—that's what they called it in 2010: the All Time Best Brewery on Earth. The Stone Brewing Company is the seventeenth largest overall brewery in the United States and the tenth largest craft brewery. (Several breweries in this book are the other nine in front of it.) The Escondido headquarters is also home to a 300-plus capacity restaurant and beer garden, and in the spring of 2013, Stone opened another brewing facility in the Point Loma neighborhood of San Diego. At over 20,000 square feet, this facility can host over 700 sud-soaked patrons at a time.

By several measures, Stone Brewing is one of the foremost leaders of craft beer you can find. But it wasn't always so—founders Steve Wagner and Greg Koch built upon their burgeoning friendship as scholars of lager at a weekend "Sensory Evaluation of Beer" conference at UC Davis in the early 1990s. They kept in touch and decided to open a brewery a few short years later using Koch's business acumen coupled with Wagner's brewing know-how. Their first full year of brewing was 1996,

and Stone's yield was about 440 barrels. The projected output for 2013 is over 200,000 barrels. Such is the power of good beer and good friends.

Like many West-Coast breweries, many of Stone's beers have a strong emphasis on hops and flavor. Several of the Stone Brewing Company's beers rate well above average in ABV, with 4 percent ABV constituting the low end of the spectrum—many beers are over 8 and even 10 percent. Stone serves nine beers on tap year round, including Stone Pale Ale (the flagship beer); Arrogant Bastard Ale, a brash American-style lager ("Hated by many. Loved by few. You're not worthy."); Stone IPA; Ruination IPA (a double IPA); and several more. Many special- and limited-edition styles and reserves are brewed and available at select times throughout the year.

The Stone Brewing Company has won six medals at the Great American Beer Festival and garnered many awards from other festivals around the United States and the world at large. In 2007, the GABF awarded a gold medal to Stone Levitation Ale in the American-Style Amber/Red Ale category. The flagship beer, Stone Pale Ale, won bronze the year before in the Extra Special Bitter or Strong Bitter category. *—Jordan Wiklund*

Nugget Nectar
Tröegs Brewing Company, Hershey, Pennsylvania

Brothers Chris and John Trogner opened Tröegs Brewing Company in 1997. Although living nearly 2,000 miles apart—one in Boulder, Colorado, and the other in Philadelphia—the two hit on a love of craft beer simultaneously. That love eventually turned into a business plan. After several years of cleaning tanks, managing restaurants, and taking classes, the plan turned into a business. The seasonal Nugget Nectar is an amped-up version of the brewery's popular HopBack Amber. It delivers a bracing pine and citrus hop wallop, tempered by an ample dose of toasty and caramel malt.

SPECIFICATIONS	OG: 1.072	FG: 1.014	ABV: 7.5%	IBU: 91	SRM: 12

Crush and steep in 2 gal. (7.5 L) of water at 152°F (67°C) for 30 minutes:

- 1.75 lb. (.8 kg) pilsner malt
- 8 oz. (225 g) Dark Munich 20L malt
- 8 oz. (225 g) Vienna malt
- 8 oz. (225 g) Crystal 60L malt

Strain the grain into your brewpot and sparge with .5 gal. (2 L) of water at 160°F (71°C). Bring the water to a boil, remove from the heat, and add:

- 6 lb. (2.72 kg) light liquid malt extract
- 26 oz. (.73 kg) light dry malt extract

Stir well until the extract is completely dissolved. Add water to bring the total volume to 3 gal. (11.3 L). Bring the wort to a rolling boil then add:

- 1.5 oz. (43 g) Nugget hop pellets (13% AA)

Boil for 60 minutes and then add:

- ½ tsp. Irish moss

Boil for 10 minutes and then add:

- .5 oz. (14.173 g) Columbus hop pellets (15% AA)

Boil for another 5 minutes and then add:

- ½ tsp. yeast nutrient

Boil for another 5 minutes and then add:

- .75 oz. (21 g) Palisade hop pellets (8.25% AA)

Boil for another 9 minutes and then add:

- 1.0 oz. (28 g) Nugget hop pellets (13% AA)
- 1.5 oz. (43 g) Simcoe hop pellets (13% AA)
- .5 oz. (14 g) Columbus hop pellets (15% AA)

Boil for 1 more minute and then chill the wort as quickly as possible to below 80°F (27°C), using an ice bath or wort chiller. Transfer the wort to the fermenter and add cold water to bring the total volume to 5 gal. (19 L). Aerate the wort. Add the yeast:

- Wyeast 1056 American Ale, WLP 001 California Ale, or Safale US-05

Ferment at 68°F (20°C) until final gravity is achieved. Siphon to a secondary fermenter and add:

- .25 oz. (7 g) Columbus hop pellets (15% AA)
- 1 oz. (28 g) Nugget hop pellets (13% AA)
- 1 oz. (28 g) Simcoe hop pellets (13% AA)

Allow the beer to condition for 7 to 10 days. Bottle when fermentation is complete with:

- 6 oz. (170 g) corn sugar

ALL-GRAIN INSTRUCTIONS

Replace the malt extract with 9.5 lbs. (4.3 kg) pilsner malt, 2.5 lbs. (1.13 kg) dark Munich malt, and 2.5 lbs. (1.13 kg) Vienna malt. Crush the grains and mash at 152°F (67°C) for 60 minutes. Sparge with 175°F (79°C) water until you reach a total volume 6.5 gallons (29.5 L) in the brewpot. Reduce the 90-minute nugget hop addition to 1.25 oz. (35 g).

THE TOWN OF HERSHEY, PENNSYLVANIA, is best known historically for its chocolate. That may change, however, with the excellent products Tröegs Brewing Company is producing.

In the future, Hershey may be known best for its beer.

Tröegs is the brainchild of brothers Chris and John Trogner. The name *Tröegs* comes from an old family nickname, from a portmanteau of the founders' surname—*Trogner*—and the Flemish word for *pub*, which is "Kroeg." Put together, Tröegs is what you get.

And *together* is a great way to describe the founders. Just eighteen months apart, Chris and John were more than 1,000 times that number apart in miles during the late 1990s, when Chris moved to Boulder, Colorado, for school and skiing, and John worked in real estate in Philadelphia. As the microbrewing scene exploded in both states, the brothers Trogner nursed the small dream of one day opening a business together. John moved to Boulder to learn the beer business, taking classes at nearby UC Davis and Chicago's Siebel Institute of Technology. Chris kept his focus on marketing and business and hopped the pond to England to take some of the best beer classes in the world at the University of Sunderland, just south of Edinburgh on the eastern coast of the United Kingdom.

In 1997, Chris and John decided to return to their native state of Pennsylvania to establish their business, and Tröegs Brewing Company has been producing beer ever since. Today, Tröegs produces six brews year-round and five seasonals, producing "handcrafted world-class beers that combine traditional English brewing techniques" with good, old-fashioned American ingenuity.

One of the most popular beers Tröegs produces is a seasonal named Nugget Nectar, an orange, hopped-up "nirvana of hops," intensifying the same malt and hop flavors that make the flagship HopBack Amber Ale so popular. At 7.5 percent ABV and rated at 93 IBU's, Nugget Nectar's seasonal availability from about February to April make it a hot commodity. In 2011, Nugget Nectar was named one of the 50 Best Beers according to www.TheFiftyBest.com, and a wide variety of Tröegs' other offerings have been perpetual Great American Beer Award winners since 2007, with a gold in every year except 2008.

Tröegs beer can be found on tap and in bottles up and down the Atlantic Coast, as well as in Ohio and Washington, D.C. Currently, there are no plans for a Hershey's chocolate beer, but that's one category Tröegs has yet to crack at the Great American Beer Festival. —*Jordan Wiklund*

Xenu
Cigar City Brewing, Tampa, Florida

This straw-colored refresher is one of the lightest offerings from Tampa's Cigar City Brewing. Light sweetness and flavors of honey and corn are balanced by bitterness that is a bit higher than normal for cream ale. European Noble hops give it a delicate, floral aroma. The honey cream ale is a thirst quencher for those hot summer days in Florida.

Daniel Wallace (Tampa Bay Times/AP Images)

SPECIFICATIONS	OG: 1.048	FG: 1.010	ABV: 5%	IBU: 24	SRM: 3

Crush and steep in 2 gal. (7.5 L) of water at 160°F (71°C) for 30 minutes:

- 14.4 oz. (408 g) flaked corn
- 8 oz. (225 g) Cara Foam malt
- 4.8 oz. (136 g) Gambrinus Honey malt

Strain the grain into your brewpot, and sparge with .5 gal. (2 L) of water at 160°F (71°C). Bring the water to a boil, remove from the heat, and add:

- 3.15 lb. (1.43 kg) pilsner liquid malt extract
- 2.25 lb. (1 kg) light dry malt extract

Stir well until the extract is completely dissolved. Add water to bring the total volume to 3 gal. (11.3 L). Bring the wort to a rolling boil, and add:

- .8 oz. (23 g) Hallertau Tradition hop pellets (6% AA)

Boil for 40 minutes, and then add:

- .33 oz. (9.4 g) Hallertau Mittelfruh hop pellets (4.5% AA)
- .25 oz. (7 g) Hallertau Tradition hop pellets (6% AA)

Boil for 20 minutes, and then add:

- .7 oz. (20 g) Czech Saaz hop pellets (3.8% AA)

Remove from the heat and chill the wort as quickly as possible to below 80°F (27°C), using an ice bath or wort chiller. Transfer the wort to the fermenter and add cold water to bring the total volume to 5 gal. (19 L). Aerate the wort. Add the yeast:

- Wyeast 1968 London ESB Ale

Ferment at 62°F (17°C) until final gravity is achieved. Siphon to a secondary fermenter and allow the beer to condition for 7 to 10 days. Bottle when fermentation is complete with:

- 6 oz. (170 g) corn sugar

ALL-GRAIN INSTRUCTIONS

Replace the malt extract with 8.75 lb. (3.97 kg) of pilsner malt. Crush the grains and mash at 152°F (67°C) for 60 minutes. Sparge with 6 gal. (22.7 L) of water at 170°F (79°C) in the brewpot. Reduce the 60-minute Hallertau Tradition hop addition to .68 oz. (19.3 g). Reduce the 20-minute Hallertau Tradition hops addition to .2 oz. (5.7 g). Reduce the 20-minute Hallertau Mittelfruh hop addition to .27 oz. (7.7 g).

Chris O'Meara (AP Images)

6 LAGERS

Don't be fooled by the mass-produced, pale-yellow brew commonly thought of as "lager beer." The world of lagers is a rich, varied, and flavorful one. While the so-called American lagers are part of the family, beyond these lie beers for people who want something more. Light-colored lager styles include the boldly bitter Bohemian and German pilsners, the maltier Munich helles, and the balanced Dortmunder export. There are the amber-colored Vienna and Märzen styles, and the smooth, black, and malty schwarzbier. Then there are the bocks. From the summery maibock to the sumptuous doppelbock, these beers display intensely rich malt that fills the mouth without being cloying.

Lagers get their name from the German verb "lagern," which means "to store." After fermentation, lager beers are kept at temperatures near freezing for periods of weeks or even months, allowing their cold-loving yeast to continue a slow cleanup process that gives these beers that crisp profile. Low-temperature fermentation by bottom-fermenting yeast strains inhibits the production of aromatic compounds like the fruity esters and spicy phenols that characterize ales. This gives lagers a clean flavor that makes even the high-test styles refreshing.

Some complain that lagers are boring, but it is a mistake to write them off so easily. Lagers are meant to be drinkable brews—beers that are content to take a backseat to the social interaction that they support. They hide their complexity under a surface of apparent simplicity. But should you choose to pay attention to them, you will be rewarded.

Lager brewing is not for beginners. Precise temperature control is a must. You will need to be able to hold the beer at a consistent low temperature for long periods of time to get the best results.

Select
Dave's BrewFarm, Wilson, Wisconsin

Dave's BrewFarm is situated in the rolling, rural landscape of western Wisconsin about 60 miles east of the Twin Cities of Minneapolis and St. Paul, Minnesota. The only thing differentiating it from the farmsteads that dot the countryside is a sign and a wind turbine atop a 120-foot tower. The "Labrewatory," as brewer David Anderson calls it, generates much of its power from the wind. Other nods to sustainability include a geothermal heat exchanger that helps heat and cool the building and planned solar panels on the roof. The BrewFarm holds frequent open-house hours, which draw people from near and far—some even camp on the acreage behind the building. While Anderson leans toward style-bending beers that feature experimental ingredients, his flagship BrewFarm Select is anything but. This is a straight-up, easy-to-drink, and flavorful take on American-style lager than boasts subtle caramel notes and moderate bitterness. And yes, he really does ferment it at 75 degrees F.

SPECIFICATIONS	OG: 1.052	FG: 1.010	ABV: 5.6%	IBU: 22	SRM: 6

Crush and steep in 1 gal. (3.8 L) of water at 160°F (71°C) for 30 minutes:

- 1.3 lb. (.6 kg) Briess Caramel 20L malt
- .65 oz. (18.42 g) Cluster hop pellets (7% AA)

Strain the grain into your brewpot and sparge with .5 gal. (2 L) of water at 160°F (71°C). Add water as needed to bring the total volume to 1.5 gal. (5.7 L). Bring the water to a boil, remove from the heat, and add:

- 6 lb. (3 kg) pilsner liquid malt extract
- 5.6 oz. (.15 kg) light dry malt extract

Stir well until the extract is completely dissolved. Add water to bring the total volume to 3 gal. (11.3 L). Bring the wort to a rolling boil. Boil for 45 minutes and then add:

- .5 oz. (14 g) Perle hop pellets (9% AA)

Chill the wort as quickly as possible to below 80°F (27°C), using an ice bath or wort chiller. Transfer the wort to the fermenter and add cold water to bring the total volume to 5 gal. (19 L). Aerate the wort. Add the yeast:

- Wyeast 2112 California Lager

Ferment at 75°F (20°C) until final gravity is achieved. Siphon to a secondary fermenter. Allow the beer to condition for 2 months at 33°F (1°C). Bottle when fermentation is complete with:

- 6 oz. (170 g) corn sugar

ALL-GRAIN INSTRUCTIONS

Replace the malt extract with 10 lb. (4.5 kg) Rahr pilsner malt. Crush the grains and mash at 152°F (66°C) for 60 minutes. Sparge with 6 gal. (22.7 L) of water at 170°F (77°C) in the brewpot. Reduce the Cluster hop addition to .5 oz. (14 g) and add pellets to the kettle as the wort is being run off.

DAVE'S BREWFARM

WILSON, WISCONSIN

THERE IS LITERALLY NO OTHER BREWPUB quite like Dave's BrewFarm. Wind-brewed beer—who'd a-thunk it?, as some native Wisconsinites might say.

That's right. Dave's BrewFarm is just that: a residential farmhouse where Dave Anderson and his wife, Pat Dixon, don't just brew beer, they brew beer using wind power, geothermal heating and cooling, and solar power. Dave's BrewFarm is a sustainability-based brewery, where more than 60 percent of the annual energy costs are accounted for through natural elements such as wind and solar power. Even the wastewater of the brewing process is recycled, turned over, and funneled into the hop yards and orchards of nearby Little Wolf Farmstead.

As of this writing, the website was under construction, so what little information was available came through the company blog (www. DavesBrewFarm.Blogspot.com), and patron reviews from websites like Yelp. From that blog, however, curious beer drinkers can find when Dave and Pat open their BrewFarm on weekends, letting the taps flow freely and inviting newcomers to the pastoral farmland setting.

The BrewFarm features an ever-changing menu of eight to ten on-tap ales and lagers. Patrons are invited to bring their own food and sit down for a while. Wilson, Wisconsin, doesn't exactly draw the beer-curious crowds the way other cities like Boulder or even nearby Minneapolis do.

Dave's Brewpub is a brewery borne of the land. Dave and Pat keep a large cache of honeybee hives for sweeter mixes, but they've been known to experiment with less traditional ingredients as well, including pomegranates, pears, and basil. And why not? They're brewing on their own farm, after all. On average, Dave has brewed about 200 to 300 barrels on site, but contracts with Steven's Point Brewery and Sand Creek Brewery as well for further distribution. The BrewFarm began in 2008 when Dave and Pat realized they had the opportunity to harvest the land's natural resources to power their brewing dreams. They have 35 acres of windswept Wisconsin farmland, where they also grow hops, herbs, blueberries, raspberries, and more.

The flagship beer is BrewFarm Select, an "easy-drinking, all-malt lager" that some unimaginative drinkers pass off as a Coors Light or Miller Lite copy. Brewmaster Anderson couldn't disagree more. He speaks passionately of its balance and flavor but recognizes that for his brewery to grow, he needs a product familiar to other beer drinkers around the state. The best way to get to know the much wider selection of Dave's BrewFarm is to simply go there. It's an experience unlike any other in the craft-brewing world. —*Jordan Wiklund*

Coney Island Mermaid Pilsner
Schmaltz Brewing, Clifton Park, New York

Coney Island Craft Lagers from Schmaltz Brewing started out life as a contract brewer but has recently opened its own 50-barrel brewery. The company is now proud to brew and bottle its "liquid curiosities" in New York. Focusing primarily on lagers, a rarity in craft beer, Coney Island produces a line of full-flavored beers. Coney Island Mermaid Pilsner features a complex grain bill, brewed in a clean pilsner style. To truly capture this beer, you will need to supplement your extracts with a partial mash. —*Matthew Schaefer*

GOLD MEDAL: BEST CRAFT BREWER IN AMERICA *- Beverage World Magazine*

MALTS: SPECIALTY 2-ROW, CARAMEL PILS, RYE ALE, CRYSTAL RYE, VIENNA, WHEAT, FLAKED OATS
HOPS: WARRIOR, AMARILLO, CRYSTAL, FUGGLE
DRY HOP: AMARILLO, CRYSTAL
5.5% ALC. BY VOL.

SILVER MEDAL WINNER
World Beer Championships

TOP 50 BREWERS IN THE WORLD
- RateBeer.com

rate**beer**

Percentile
96
style

SPECIFICATIONS	OG: 1.051	FG: 1.010	ABV: 5.2%	IBU: 25	SRM: 5

Crush and steep in 2 gal. (7.57 L) of water at 162°F (72°C) for 60 minutes to reach a mash temperature of 150°F (66°C):

- 2 lb. (.9 kg) Vienna malt
- 1 lb. (.45 kg) Carapils
- 8 oz. (227 g) flaked oats
- 8 oz. (227 g) wheat malt
- 8 oz. (227 g) rye malt

Strain the grain into your brewpot and add:

- .63 oz. (18 g) Crystal hop pellets (4.5% AA)
- .32 oz. (9 g) Amarillo hop pellets (9.5% AA)
- .32 oz. (9 g) Tettnang hop pellets (4.5% AA)

Sparge with 3 gal. (11.35 L) of water at 168°F (75.6°C). Bring the water to a boil, remove from the heat, and add:

- 4 lb. (1.8 kg) pilsner liquid extract

Stir well until the extract is completely dissolved. Add water to bring the total volume to 4.25 gal. (16.1 L). Bring the wort to a rolling boil and boil for 75 minutes.

Remove from the heat and add:

- .5 oz. (14 g) Amarillo hop pellets (9.5% AA)
- .5 oz. (14 g) Crystal hop pellets (4.5% AA)

Chill the wort as quickly as possible to below 80°F (27°C), using an ice bath or wort chiller. (The closer you can get to the fermentation temperature of 50°F [10°C] the better.) Transfer the wort to the fermenter and add cold water to bring the total volume to 5 gal. (19 L). Aerate the wort. Add the yeast:

- Wyeast 2124 Bohemian Lager

Ferment at 50°F (10°C) until specific gravity reaches 1.015 and then raise the temperature to 70°F (21°C) for a diacetyl rest until final gravity is achieved. Siphon to a secondary fermenter and add:

- .5 oz. (14 g) Amarillo hop pellets (9.5% AA)
- .5 oz. (14 g) Crystal hop pellets (4.5% AA)

Allow the beer to condition for 7 days before removing the dry hops and cold conditioning as close to freezing as possible for 2 months before bottling. When bottling, reintroduce a small amount of active yeast along with:

- 5 oz. (140 g) corn sugar

ALL-GRAIN INSTRUCTIONS

Replace the grain bill above with the following and steep at 150°F (66°C) for 60 minutes. Sparge with water at 170°F (77°C) to achieve a volume of 6 gal. (22.7 L) in the kettle. The hop bill remains the same:

- 8.5 lb. (3.86 kg) two-row pale malt
- 1 lb. (.45 kg) Vienna malt
- 8 oz. (227g) Carapils
- 8 oz. (227 g) rye malt
- 4 oz. (113 g) wheat malt
- 4 oz. (113 g) flaked oats
- 2 oz. (57 g) Crystal rye

Schell's Pils
August Schell Brewing Company, New Ulm, Minnesota

August Schell Brewing Company is the second-oldest family-owned brewery in the United States. For more than 150 years it has remained true to its founder's roots by brewing high-quality examples of traditional German lagers and ales. Schell's Pils is one of the company's best. It has won accolades in national and international competition, including gold, silver, and bronze medals at the Great American Beer Festival. The late beer writer Michael Jackson called it, "one of the best American examples of the Pilsner style." Sharp and peppery, it puts spicy German hops at the forefront with light, grainy-sweet malt to provide support.

SPECIFICATIONS	OG: 1.051	FG: 1.013	ABV: 5%	IBU: 38	SRM: 3

Crush and steep in .5 gal. (2 L) of water at 160°F (71°C) for 30 minutes:

- 3.5 oz. (99 g) Carapils malt
- .62 oz. (17.57 g) Sterling hop pellets (5.5% AA)

Strain the grain into your brewpot and sparge with .5 gal. (2 L) of water at 160°F (71°C). Add water to bring the volume to 2 gal. (7.5 L). Bring to a boil, remove from the heat, and add:

- 6 lb. (2.7 kg) pilsner liquid malt extract
- 12 oz. (340 g) light dry malt extract

Stir well until the extract is completely dissolved. Add water to bring the total volume to 3 gal. (11.3 L). Bring the wort to a rolling boil then add:

- .56 oz. (15.87 g) Sterling hop pellets (5.5% AA)

Boil for 40 minutes and then add:

- .77 oz. (21.83 g) Sterling hop pellets (5.5% AA)

Boil for 15 minutes and then add:

- 1.55 oz. (43.94 g) Sterling hop pellets (5.5% AA)

Boil for 5 more minutes. Remove from the heat and chill the wort as quickly as possible to below 80°F (27°C), using an ice bath or wort chiller. Transfer the wort to the fermenter and add cold water to bring the total volume to 5 gal. (19 L). Aerate the wort. Add the yeast:

- Wyeast 2000 Budvar Lager

Ferment at 50°F (10°C) until final gravity is achieved. Siphon to a secondary fermenter and add:

- 1.25 oz. (35.4 g) Sterling hop pellets (5.5% AA)

Allow the beer to condition for 3 weeks at 33°F (1°C). Bottle when fermentation is complete with:

- 6 oz. (170 g) corn sugar

ALL-GRAIN INSTRUCTIONS

Replace the malt extract with 10.7 lb. (4.85 kg) of two-row pale malt. Crush the grains and mash at 144° F (62° C) for 40 minutes. Raise the temperature to 158°F (70°C) and rest for 10 minutes. Raise the temperature to 170°F (79°C). Sparge with with water at 170°F (79°C) until you reach a total volume of 6 gallons (22.7 L) in the brewpot. Reduce the first Sterling hop addition to .54 oz. (15.31 g). Reduce the 60-minute Sterling hop addition to .48 oz. (13.6 g). Reduce the 20-minute Sterling hop addition to .66 oz. (18.7 g). Reduce the 5-minute Sterling hop addition to 1.34 oz. (38 g).

GLOSSARY OF BEER TERMS

A

ABV Alcohol by volume, the measurement of the alcohol content in beer expressed as a percentage of the total volume.

ABW Alcohol by weight, the measurement of the alcohol content in beer expressed as a percentage of the total weight.

adjunct Any nonenzymatic fermentable sugar. Adjuncts include syrups, refined sugars, and unmalted cereals such as flaked barley or corn grits.

ale Typically refers to beers fermented with top-fermenting yeast strains and at higher temperatures, commonly between 65 and 75°F (18 and 24°C). Fermentation at higher temperatures promotes the formation by yeast of various flavor and aromatic compounds, including esters and phenols, that give beer fruity and spicy flavors.

aerate To mix air into a solution to provide oxygen for yeast. Brewers must aerate wort before fermentation for healthy yeast growth.

aerobic Describes any process that takes place in the presence of oxygen. Yeast fermentation begins as an aerobic process and then changes to an anaerobic one.

aroma The fragrance that emanates from beer. Beer aroma comes from malt, hop oils, and various byproducts of fermentation.

alpha acids The chemical compounds in hops that, when isomerized by boiling, give bitterness to beer.

anaerobic Describes a process that takes place in the absence of oxygen or which may require its absence. Yeast fermentation begins as an aerobic process and then changes to an anaerobic one.

attenuation The degree of conversion of sugar to alcohol and CO_2 through fermentation. Beers with a low degree of attenuation will be full-bodied with higher levels of residual sugar. Higher attenuated beers will be drier and lighter bodied.

B

balance A beer's proportion of malt flavor and sweetness to hop flavor and bitterness.

barrel A volume measurement of beer. A U.S. barrel equals thirty-one U.S. gallons. The most common keg size is a half-barrel, which contains fifteen and a half U.S. gallons.

beer A fermented beverage made from cereal grains.

beer engine A hand pump that pulls cask-conditioned beer up from the cask.

boiling The stage of the brewing process in which wort is boiled to isomerize hop alpha acids, dissolve hop essential oils, and coagulate and remove proteins that cause haze in the finished beer.

bottle-conditioned Refers to beers that have been naturally carbonated by refermentation in the bottle. Bottle-conditioned beers usually have a thin sediment of yeast at the bottom of the bottle that should be left behind when pouring.

bottom-fermenting A reference to the tendency of yeast to flocculate at the bottom of the fermenter at the end of fermentation. Usually refers to lager yeasts.

budding The asexual means of reproduction by yeast in which "daughter" cells split off from the original cell.

C

cask-conditioned Refers to beer that has been refermented in a keg, usually a firkin, to create natural carbonation. Cask-conditioned beers are typically poured by gravity or pulled to the faucet with a pump rather than being pushed with CO_2. They are usually served at cellar temperature and have lower levels of carbonation than draft beer. Also called "real ale."

cellar temperature A temperature between 48 and 55 degrees F (9 and 13 degrees C). The correct serving temperature for most ales.

caramelization A chemical degradation of sugar through heat in which the sugar is converted to caramel.

conditioning A period of time during which beer is allowed to mature. Conditioning imparts natural carbonation, develops flavor, and clarifies the beer by allowing suspended yeast and proteins to drop out.

contract brewing A situation in which beer is brewed by one brewery and marketed by another. Most often the receiving entity is a "beer marketing company" that does not own a brewery. In some cases breweries contract some brewing to others when their own capacity is not great enough to fill demand.

craft brewer The Brewers Association, a trade group representing the brewing industry, defines a craft brewer as

Small: producing less than six million barrels of beer annually

Independent: less than 25 percent ownership by an entity that is not a craft brewer

Traditional: has an all-malt flagship beer or at least 50 percent of its volume in beer is made with only malt or uses adjuncts such as corn or rice only to enhance flavor

D

decoction mashing A traditional German process in which a portion of the grain is removed from the mash tun, boiled, and then returned to the main mash. It is used to ensure maximum starch conversion and to develop rich malt character. Modern, highly modified malts have made decoction mashing less necessary.

degrees Plato An alternative scale to measure the amount of sugar in wort by measuring the refraction of light passing through it. A specific gravity of 1.040 equals approximately 10° Plato.

diacetyl A volatile compound produced by yeast during fermentation. While it is a desirable component of some beer styles in small amounts, in most beers, and at higher concentrations, it is generally considered a flaw. The flavor of diacetyl is commonly compared to butter or butterscotch.

diastatic power The amount of diastatic enzyme potential that a malt contains. Diastatic enzymes break down complex starches into simpler sugars. It is through diastatic enzyme activity that brewers convert the starches in barley to fermentable sugars during the mash step of the brewing process.

dry hopping Adding hops to fermenting or conditioning beer to increase hop flavor and aroma.

E

enzymes Protein-based catalysts that affect specific biochemical reactions. Diastatic enzymes break down complex starches into simpler sugars.

essential oils The volatile compounds in hops that, when dissolved in beer, provide flavors and aromas.

esters Aromatic compounds formed from alcohols by yeast action. Typically fruity.

F

final gravity (FG) A measurement of the remaining sugar content of beer following fermentation that is based on the density of the fluid.

firkin An English quarter-barrel keg. A firkin contains nine imperial gallons. Commonly used for cask-conditioned beer.

flocculation The state of being clumped together. For yeast, the clumping and settling out of a solution after fermentation has completed.

G

gelatinization The process of rendering starches soluble in water by heat or a combination of heat and enzyme action. In making beer, the starches in grains must be gelatinized for the enzymatic conversion to fermentable sugars to occur.

germination The stage of plant growth during which the seed puts forth a sprout. Germination is the first step in the malting process.

grain bill The list of grains used in a beer recipe.

grist The term for milled grain prior to the mashing step of the brewing process.

growler A large jar or jug, usually a half gallon, for taking home beer from a brewery or a brewpub.

gruit A beer that is flavored and made bitter with a mixture of herbs and spices. Also refers to the spice mix itself.

H

hop back A vessel filled with hops that acts as a filter, removing coagulated proteins from wort on the way to the chiller. As hot wort flows through the hop back, it dissolves essential oils from the hops that give hop aroma to the beer.

hops The cone-like flowers of the perennial vine *Humulus lupulus*. Used in beer, hops provide bitterness, flavor, and aroma. They also have preservative properties that can help extend the shelf-life of beer.

I

IBU International Bittering Unit. A chemical measurement of the actual bitterness in beer. An IBU is defined as one milligram of isomerized alpha acid per liter of beer. May be different from perceived bitterness.

infusion mashing The process in which grains are soaked in water of a specified temperature for a specified period of time to activate enzymes that convert starches to sugars. The grains are not boiled. For a single-infusion mash, all of the water is added at one time and the grains are allowed to soak at a constant temperature. In a stepped-infusion mash, a portion of the water is held back and heated to a higher temperature. When added to the mash tun it raises the temperature of the grains by carefully controlled degrees.

IPA India pale ale. A beer style developed in England in the eighteenth century for export to India. Higher alcoholic strength and higher levels of hopping helped the beer survive the five-month sea voyage. The style has become one of the most popular among American craft-beer drinkers.

isomerization A chemical process in which a compound is changed into another form with the same chemical composition but a different structure. Alpha acids in hops must be isomerized to impart bitterness in beer.

K

kreusen The foamy head of yeast, proteins, and hop resins that forms on beer during peak fermentation.

kreusening The practice of adding a small amount of fermenting wort to conditioning beer. The intent is to create natural carbonation through secondary fermentation.

L

lager Typically refers to beers that are fermented with bottom-fermenting yeast strains at cooler temperatures, commonly between 48 and 55 degrees F (9 and 13 degrees C). Fermentation at colder temperatures inhibits the production by yeast of various flavor and aromatic compounds, resulting in beers with a crisp, clean flavor profile. Lagers are typically conditioned at temperatures near freezing for periods of weeks to months.

Lovibond A unit of malt color measurement based on standardized colored solutions. Malt color is measured in degrees Lovibond. Lower numbers are lighter colored and higher numbers are darker.

lupulin glands Small, bright yellow nodes at the base of each hop petal that contain the alpha acids and essential oils used by brewers.

M

malt A cereal grain, usually barley, that has gone through the malting process to begin the breakdown of starches into simpler sugars. The malting process includes germination, drying, and kilning to various degrees of color and flavor intensity. Other malted grains commonly used in beer include wheat, oats, and rye.

malt extract Malt in the form of concentrated powder or syrup that is dissolved in water to make wort.

mashing The stage of the brewing process in which cereal grains are steeped in water to activate enzymes that break down the complex starches into simple sugars that are fermentable by yeast. Mashing occurs in a vessel called a mash tun.

Maillard reaction A browning reaction caused by external heat wherein a sugar and an amino acid form a complex. Maillard reactions occurring during the kilning stage of the malting process yield grains that impart amber to brown color and toasty, caramel flavor compounds called melanoidins in the finished beer.

modification The degree to which the starches in grain are enzymatically degraded and simplified during the germination step of the malting process. Although brewers desire highly modified malt to achieve maximum efficiency in the conversion of starches to sugar during the mash step of brewing, modification must be stopped before all of the starch has been degraded.

mouthfeel A description of how beer feels in the mouth. Mouthfeel includes considerations such as body, texture, alcoholic warmth, and carbonation.

O

original gravity (OG) A measurement of the sugar content of wort prior to fermentation based on the density of the fluid.

oxidation The exposure of beer to oxygen. Oxidation may cause stale or cardboard flavors. In some stronger beers the effects of oxidation can be favorable, giving a sherry-like character.

P

phenols A class of aromatic compounds formed by yeast during fermentation. Typically spicy or smoky, phenols can also taste medicinal. Phenols are often considered a flaw, but in some beers a bit of clove-like phenolic character is an essential part of the style.

pitching Adding yeast to wort.

R

racking Moving beer or wort from one brewing vessel to another.

randall A hop-filled vessel that is placed in the draft line between the keg and the faucet.

real ale Beer that has been refermented in the keg, usually a firkin, to create natural carbonation. Cask-conditioned beers are typically poured by gravity or pulled to the faucet with a pump rather than being pushed with CO_2. They are usually served at cellar temperature and have lower levels of carbonation than draft beer. Also called "cask-conditioned."

Reinheitsgebot The Bavarian purity law dating to 1516 that permits only three ingredients in the making of beer: barley malt, hops, and water.

S

session beer A beer, usually with a low-alcohol content, that allows one to drink several in one sitting without becoming inebriated or "full."

sparging The process of spraying spent grains with water at the end of the mash in order to rinse out any sugars that remain when the wort is drained from the mash tun.

specific gravity (SG) A measure of the malt sugar concentration of wort or beer based on the density of the fluid. The specific gravity of water is 1.000 at 59°F (15°C). Typical original gravities for beer fall between 1.035 and 1.060.

SRM Standard reference method: a method for measuring color in beer. Lower numbers represent a lighter color and higher numbers a darker color.

T

top-fermenting A reference to the tendency of yeast to flocculate at the top of the fermenter at the end of fermentation. It usually refers to ale yeasts.

trub The sediment at the bottom of a fermenter. Pronounced "troob."

W

wort The term for unfermented beer. Pronounced "wert."

Y

yeast A class of unicellular fungi. During fermentation yeast metabolizes sugar and converts it into alcohol, carbon dioxide, and an assortment of other aromatic and flavor compounds that include esters and phenols. Brewing yeasts fall into the family *Saccharomyces*. Top-fermenting ale yeasts are of the species *Saccharomyces cerevisiae*. Bottom-fermenting lager yeast is *Saccharomyces pastorianus*.

INDEX

Bold numbers indicate a recipe or brewery profile.

CONTRIBUTORS

Michael Agnew is a Certified Cicerone® and national-level Beer Judge Certification Program (BJCP) judge based in the booming beertropolis of Minneapolis, Minnesota. With his company, A Perfect Pint, Michael leads beer tastings, beer dinners, and beer education events for corporate and private clients at venues throughout the Twin Cities and beyond. He pens a monthly beer column for the *Minneapolis Star Tribune*, and his beer musings can also be found on Seriouseats.com, *The Growler* magazine, his own A Perfect Pint blog, and the Hop Press at Ratebeer.com, among other outlets. Michael is the author of *A Prairie Beer Companion: Brews, Breweries, and Brewpubs of the Heartland*, a guide to the breweries and brewpubs of Minnesota, Wisconsin, Iowa, and Illinois.

Billy Broas is the founder of The Homebrew Academy, an online training website for homebrewers with thousands of members worldwide. He is also the homebrewing expert in the Rocky Mountain PBS television show *Colorado Brews*. Billy started brewing beer in college and hasn't slowed down. Billy also blogs about craft beer culture at BillyBrew.com.

Denny Conn brewed his first batch of homebrew in 1998 and since then has brewed more than 400 batches. He is a Beer Judge Certification Program National–ranked beer judge and has been a member of the Governing Committee of the American Homebrewers Association for nine years. He is known for his Rye IPA recipe, which has been brewed by several commercial breweries both in the United States and Europe. He is the developer of the Cheap'n'Easy all-grain brewing system and lives in the foothills of the Coast Range in Oregon with his wife, five cats, and two dogs.

Matthew Schaefer has been homebrewing for over 15 years and is the author of *The Illustrated Guide to Brewing Beer: A Comprehensive Handboook of Beginning Home Brewing*. He is also one of the charter members and vice-president of Brewstoria, the only hombrewing club in Queens New York, where he lives with his wife, Kimberly, and his son, Evan.

Jordan Wiklund is a writer and editor from St. Paul, Minnesota, and an unrepentant IPA man through and through. His work has appeared in *[Pank]* , *Brevity*, *Versus*, *Fourth Genre*,and *The Believer* literary magazines. He is also a contributing editor to Minneapolis' own *Paper Darts* literary magazine and a proud member of the St. Paul Curling Club. Find him on Twitter @JordanWiklund.

ACKNOWLEDGMENTS

Dave Anderson, Dave's BrewFarm

Adam Avery and Joe Osborn, Avery Brewing Company

Jesse Cutler, Shmaltz Brewing Company

Kevin Eichelberger, Red Eye Brewing Company

Jeff Erway, La Cumbre Brewing Company

Mallika Filtz, Epic Brewing Company

Mitch Hamilton, Blue Mountain Brewery

Todd Haug, Surly Brewing Company

Andrew Hood, Tallgrass Brewing Company

Amanda Johnson, Odell Brewing Company

Ron Lindenbusch and Jeremy Marshall,

    Lagunitas Brewing Company

Steve Lonsway, Stone Cellar Brewpub

Sabrina LoPiccolo, Stone Brewing Company

John Maier, Rogue Ales

Jace Marti and Dave Berg,

    August Schell Brewing Company

Nick Nunns, TRVE Brewing

Jason Perkins, Allagash Brewing Company

Joey Redner, Cigar City Brewing

Ted Rice, Marble Brewery

Patrick Rue, The Bruery

Gordon Schuck, Funkwerks

Chris and John Trogner, Tröegs Brewing Company

Matt Van Wyk, Oakshire Brewing

. . . and **Bryan Stusse** for photo research.